Southern Living
what's for supper

5 Ingredient Weeknight Meals

Oxmoor House®

Grilled Sirloin Steaks and Onions, p 21

Apple and Goat Cheese Pizza, p 100

Summer Fresh Ratatouille, p 220

Cream-Filled Pound Cake, p 236

welcome

Family and friends often ask me, "How do you pull off cooking a from-scratch meal every night of the week?" As a busy, working mom, I don't always have time to shop for recipes with long and complicated ingredient lists. That's why I've created *What's for Supper 5-Ingredient Weeknight Meals*—dinners using only a handful of ingredients that save you both time and money. By stocking your pantry with basics, such as a variety of oils, vinegars, and condiments, all you need is a few extra fresh ingredients. Plus, every recipe is ready in 30 minutes or less, so you can get dinner on the table in a hurry—it's faster than ordering pizza!

In Hot Off the Grill, a quick marinade of soy sauce, fresh ginger, sesame oil, and brown sugar packs flavor into Korean Flank Steak (page 19). In Pastas and Pizzas, precooked beef and fresh pizza dough from the grocery store make Philly Cheesesteak Pizza (page 86) a breeze. Mix up the dinner routine with a tasty Smoked Salmon, Goat Cheese, and Asparagus Frittata (page 140) in Not Just for Breakfast and a crisp green salad. My meat-and-potatoes-loving family raves about the Pulled-Pork Shepherd's Pie (page 169) in Dinner in a Dish.

Don't miss From My Kitchen tips, where I've shared my *Southern Living* Test Kitchen expertise through easy ingredient swaps and savvy technique secrets. You'll learn how to perfectly toast hamburger buns and how to trim asparagus before cooking. I've also included Budget Special tips to show you how to shop smart and save big at the grocery store.

In my home kitchen, my 12-year-old son Matthew loves to lend a hand, whether it's assembling lasagna or mixing up a big salad. Through cooking together, I've taught my little helper one very important lesson— a home-cooked meal is always better than fast food. For me, nothing tops the simple pleasure of sharing a delicious meal with my family.

Vanessa McNeil Rocchio

Vanessa McNeil Rocchio
Southern Living Test Kitchen

contents

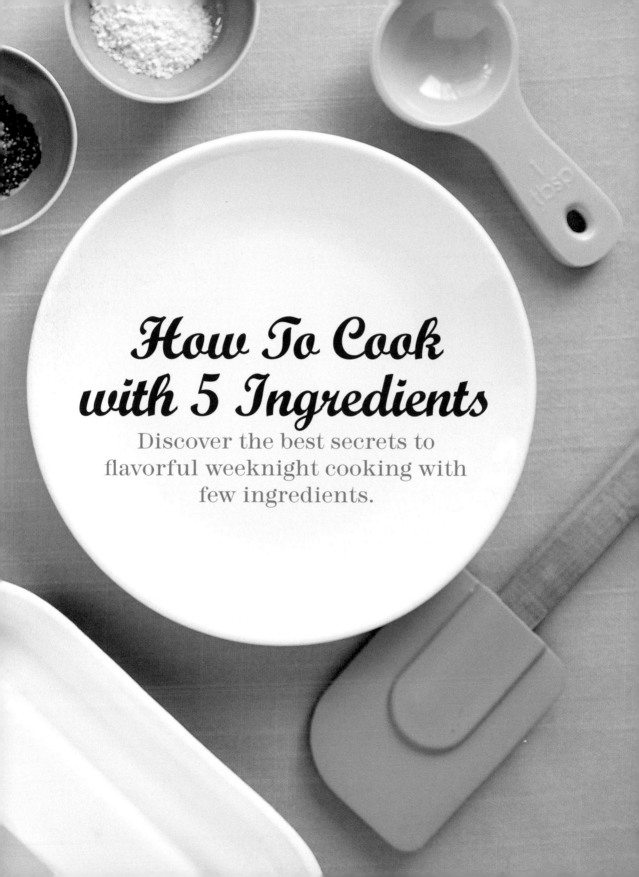

How To Cook with 5 Ingredients

Discover the best secrets to flavorful weeknight cooking with few ingredients.

The Basic
5-Ingredient Pantry

I'll let you in on a little secret. The key to making these quick, 5-ingredient recipes is to keep your pantry and fridge stocked with these basics. If you have these simple ingredients then you can use them to make any of our recipes. These ingredients are not included in our ingredient count.

1. Oils
vegetable, olive, canola, and cooking spray

2. Salt and Pepper
sea, kosher, and table salt; white and freshly ground pepper

3. Vinegars
red wine, rice, white, and apple cider

4. Sugar
granulated and brown

5. Sauces
Worcestershire and soy

6. Dry Baking Ingredients
flour, baking soda, and baking powder

7. Condiments
mayonnaise, yellow mustard, and ketchup

8. Other
honey and butter

Flavorful
5-Ingredient Cooking

Yes, it is possible to enjoy a delicious, home-cooked meal using just 5 ingredients. Fewer ingredients actually pull out the brilliant flavors of the food. Here are our best tips for fast, flavorful cooking with few ingredients.

1. Look for Quality
Since you only need 5 ingredients, be sure to buy the highest quality that you can for the best flavor.

2. Add Flavor to Soups and Stir-fries
Add whole wheat or plain potato gnocchi to a stir-fry or soup for added flavor.

3. Make Tasty Sandwiches
Try sandwiches for a quick, perfect 5-ingredient dinner. Jazz them up using frozen waffles that can easily turn into a sandwich with the help of a panini press.

4. Try Frozen Ingredients
Cut ingredients and make meal planning a breeze with the plethora of steam-in-bag veggies, frozen and fresh, available in the grocery store.

5. Buy the Right Meat
Look for precooked/preseasoned meats, poultry, and fish/shellfish at your supermarket, such as rotisserie chicken, steamed shrimp, or refrigerated beef roast.

6. Purchase in Season
Cook what's in season to bring out the freshest flavors in the food.

7. Incorporate Great Taste
Look for ingredients that have 2 flavor profiles to add more taste to your dish without more ingredients.

8. Try Some Cheese
Add fresh flavor to your recipes with rich-flavored cheese. Parmesan, Havarti, blue cheese, and goat cheese are all great choices.

9. Grill for Flavor
Pull out the grill for a simple way to intensify the natural flavor of foods. In fact, we devote an entire chapter to this quick-cooking method.

10. Experiment with Herbs
Infuse flavor into your dishes by using fresh herbs. To keep them fresh for up to a week, trim about ¼ inch from the stems, and rinse with cold water. Loosely wrap herbs in a damp paper towel; then seal them in a zip-top plastic bag filled with air.

10 Time-Saving Tips

Give yourself an even bigger time
advantage with some of our fastest hints.

1. Speed Up Cooking Time
Heat broth in the microwave while you are prepping
ingredients for a soup, and then add the hot broth to the
pan to speed up cooking time.

2. Keep a Key Ingredient On Hand
Keep precooked meatballs, such as Mama Lucia or Aidells,
on hand because they heat up quickly and can then be made
into sandwiches or Italian dishes.

3. Use Garlic Paste
Use garlic paste. It's easy to squeeze into a dish to add flavor,
and you don't need to get out a knife or cutting board.

4. Shop Smart
Ask the seafood department to peel shrimp or take skin off
fish fillets, ask the butcher to cut meat into the portions
for a recipe, and buy precut veggies from the grocery store
salad bar. That way when you get home during the week,
you don't have to mess with your ingredients.

5. Boil Water Faster
To bring water to a boil more quickly, preheat the pan on the stove, start with hot tap water, and cover the pot until the water reaches the boiling point.

6. Use Prepackaged Goodness
Eliminate chopping and slicing vegetables by using packaged prechopped vegetables from the produce section of your supermarket.

7. Discover a Well-Stocked Secret
Keep your pantry, fridge, and freezer well stocked with commonly used food items to avoid last-minute shopping trips for missing ingredients.

8. Think Small
Slice larger cuts of meats like pork tenderloin into medallions or thin strips to shorten cooking times.

9. Put It Together
Gather all of the ingredients before you begin cooking.

10. Make the Most of Your Time
While you wait for the oven to preheat or water to boil, prep the ingredients.

Equip Your Kitchen

A kitchen stocked with the right time-saving tools and appliances makes cooking so much easier. These are the 5 must-haves for 5-ingredient meals.

1. Garlic Press
Use a garlic press when a recipe calls for crushed or minced garlic. This tool provides the easiest and most efficient method for crushing garlic, and it can be used instead of mincing garlic with a knife.

2. Kitchen Shears
Use a pair of kitchen shears for small mincing or chopping jobs instead of pulling out a knife and cutting board. Kitchen shears are ideal for a variety of tasks—from snipping herbs and chopping canned vegetables in the can to chopping dried fruit and trimming fat from chicken breasts.

3. Flat-Sided Meat Mallet
Cut the cook time and produce tender and moist chicken-breast dishes by using a flat-sided meat mallet. Just place skinless, boneless chicken breasts between two layers of heavy-duty plastic wrap, and pound to an even thickness—about ¼ to ½ inch thick.

4. Extra Measuring Cups and Spoons
Select a set of metal or plastic measuring cups for dry ingredients. They come in sizes of 1 cup, ½ cup, ⅓ cup, and ¼ cup. Measuring spoons also come in plastic or metal and graduate in size from ⅛ teaspoon to 1 tablespoon. Keeping multiple sets on hand makes cooking faster.

5. Food Processor
Use it to chop several batches of vegetables at one time, and freeze them for later use.

Hot Off the Grill

Fire up the coals to prepare
a flavorful dinner
the whole family will love.

BBQ Bacon Burgers

MAKES: 4 SERVINGS   **HANDS-ON TIME:** 17 MIN.
TOTAL TIME: 17 MIN.

Grill a sliced Vidalia onion on the grill alongside the burgers for an extra topping. Lettuce, tomato, and pickles would also pair well with these burgers.

1½	lb. ground round	4	slices white Cheddar cheese
¼	tsp. table salt	4	sesame seed hamburger buns
¼	tsp. freshly ground pepper	8	cooked bacon slices
½	cup barbecue sauce, divided		

1. Preheat grill to 350° to 400° (medium-high) heat. Shape beef into 4 (4-inch diameter) patties. Sprinkle with salt and pepper.

2. Place patties on cooking grate of grill; brush with 2 tbsp. barbecue sauce. Grill, covered with grill lid, 5 minutes. Turn patties over; brush with an additional 2 tbsp. barbecue sauce. Cook 5 minutes or until beef is no longer pink in center. Top each burger with 1 slice cheese. Grill, covered with grill lid, 1 minute or until cheese melts.

3. Place 1 patty on bottom half of each bun. Top each with bacon and barbecue sauce. Top with bun.

From My Kitchen
Toast buns on grill; a swipe of melted butter makes them crispy.

Korean Flank Steak

MAKES: 6 SERVINGS   **HANDS-ON TIME:** 3 MIN.
TOTAL TIME: 8 HOURS, 7 MIN.

¼ cup firmly packed
   light brown sugar
¼ cup soy sauce
2 tsp. dark sesame oil
1 tsp. grated fresh ginger

¼ tsp. table salt
2 (l-lb.) flank steaks
Cooking spray
Garnish: sliced green onions

1. Combine first 5 ingredients in a shallow dish or large zip-top plastic freezer bag; add steaks. Cover or seal, and chill 8 hours.

2. Preheat grill to 450° (high) heat. Remove steaks from marinade, discarding marinade. Coat steaks with cooking spray. Grill steak, covered with grill lid, 2 minutes on each side or to desired degree of doneness. Remove from grill, and let stand 5 minutes. Cut steak diagonally across the grain into thin slices.

From My Kitchen

Serve this Asian-flavored steak alongside rice and steamed broccoli for a quick weeknight meal.

Grilled Sirloin Steaks and Onions

MAKES: 4 SERVINGS **HANDS-ON TIME:** 8 MIN.
TOTAL TIME: 28 MIN.

Brighten up classic steak seasoning with fresh rosemary or other fresh herb for seasoning steaks.

1	tsp. Montreal steak seasoning	1	medium-size red onion, cut into ¼-inch-thick slices
1	tsp. chopped fresh rosemary	2	Tbsp. olive oil
4	(6-oz.) top sirloin steaks	4	tsp. balsamic glaze
			Garnish: arugula leaves

1. Preheat grill to 350° to 400° (medium-high) heat. Combine steak seasoning and rosemary in a small bowl. Brush steaks and onion slices with olive oil. Rub steaks with rosemary mixture.

2. Grill steaks, covered with grill lid, 5 to 6 minutes on each side or to desired degree of doneness. Remove from grill; cover with aluminum foil, and let stand 10 minutes.

3. Meanwhile, grill onion, covered with grill lid, 5 minutes on each side or until tender; remove from grill. Cut onion slices crosswise in half. Serve on top of steak. Drizzle each serving with 1 tsp. balsamic glaze.

Budget Special
Sirloin provides great flavor at a great value. It's an excellent choice for fast cooking.

Grilled Pork Tenderloins with Plums

MAKES: 6 SERVINGS **HANDS-ON TIME:** 10 MIN.
TOTAL TIME: 34 MIN.

Cooking spray
2 (1-lb.) pork tenderloins
2 Tbsp. olive oil
3 plums, cut in half and pitted
1 tsp. table salt
½ tsp. freshly ground pepper
½ cup plum preserves
3 Tbsp. balsamic vinegar
1 tsp. fresh thyme leaves
Garnish: fresh thyme leaves

1. Coat a cold cooking grate with cooking spray, and place on grill. Preheat grill to 350° to 400° (medium-high) heat. Rub pork with olive oil. Sprinkle pork and plum halves with salt and pepper.

2. Whisk together plum preserves, balsamic vinegar, and thyme in a small bowl until blended. Reserve ⅓ cup preserves mixture for later use.

3. Place pork on cooking grate; baste with about 3 Tbsp. remaining preserve mixture. Grill, covered with grill lid, 18 to 20 minutes or until a meat thermometer inserted in thickest portion registers 155°, turning over and basting with remaining 2 Tbsp. preserve mixture halfway through. Remove pork from grill; let stand 10 to 12 minutes or until thermometer registers 160°. Grill plum halves 2 to 3 minutes on each side or until grill marks appear.

4. Cut pork crosswise into slices, and serve with plum halves and reserved ⅓ cup preserves mixture.

Budget Special
Buy plums in season, and freeze to use later.

Grilled Pork Chops with Tomatillo Salsa

MAKES: 4 SERVINGS **HANDS-ON TIME:** 17 MIN.
TOTAL TIME: 17 MIN.

Bone-in chops tend to be juicier and more tender than boneless chops, which results in more flavor.

4	(2-inch-thick) bone-in pork, center-cut pork loin chops
2	Tbsp. olive oil
1	tsp. table salt, divided
¼	tsp. freshly ground pepper
7	fresh tomatillos, husks removed
1	small onion, cut into ½-inch slices
2	Tbsp. chopped fresh cilantro
2	Tbsp. fresh lime juice
Garnish: fresh cilantro	

1. Preheat grill to 350° to 400° (medium-high) heat. Rub pork chops with olive oil; sprinkle with ½ tsp. salt and pepper.

2. Grill pork, tomatillos, and onion slices, covered with grill lid, 5 minutes on each side or until or until a thermometer inserted into thickest portion of each chop registers 145° and vegetables are tender.

3. Process tomatillos, onion slices, cilantro, lime juice, and remaining ½ tsp. salt in a food processor 10 to 20 seconds or until slightly chunky. Serve salsa over pork chops.

From My Kitchen

Look for tomatillos that are all about the same size for more even cooking. The smaller ones have a sweeter flavor.

Mustard Rosemary Pork Kabobs

MAKES: 6 SERVINGS   **HANDS-ON TIME:** 25 MIN.
TOTAL TIME: 1 HOUR, 25 MIN.

⅓ cup savory Dijon-style
   honey mustard
1 Tbsp. chopped fresh
   rosemary
2 Tbsp. olive oil
1 tsp. garlic salt
½ tsp. freshly ground pepper
2 (¾-lb.) pork tenderloins,
   cut into 2-inch cubes

Cooking spray
4 red bell peppers, cut
   into 2-inch pieces
1 (8-oz.) package fresh
   mushrooms
6 (8-inch) metal skewers
Garnish: chopped fresh
   rosemary

From My Kitchen

Marinate pork and prepare
veggies the night before. The next
day, just preheat the grill while you
thread the skewers. Dinner will
be on the grill in no time.

1. Place first 5 ingredients in large zip-top plastic freezer bag. Seal
bag, and shake to blend. Add pork to bag. Seal bag, and chill 1 hour.

2. Coat a cold cooking grate with cooking spray, and place on grill.
Preheat grill to 350° to 400° (medium-high) heat. Remove pork
from marinade, discarding marinade. Thread pork and vegetables
evenly onto skewers.

3. Grill skewers, covered with grill lid, 12 minutes,
turning halfway through.

Ginger Pork Chops with Grilled Peach Relish

MAKES: 4 SERVINGS **HANDS-ON TIME:** 26 MIN.
TOTAL TIME: 4 HOURS, 26 MIN.

½ cup red pepper jelly
¼ cup soy sauce
3 Tbsp. canola oil
2 Tbsp. grated fresh ginger
½ tsp. garlic salt
4 (14-oz.) bone-in pork loin chops (1¼ inches thick)

Cooking spray
1 medium-size red onion, cut into ½-inch-thick slices
4 peaches, halved
1 Tbsp. apple cider vinegar

Budget Special
When buying peaches, local is ideal. Look for fruit that is not bruised.

1. Whisk together first 5 ingredients in a bowl; reserve 3 Tbsp. for later use. Pour marinade into a large shallow dish or zip-top plastic freezer bag; add pork, turning to coat. Cover or seal, and chill 4 hours, turning occasionally. Remove pork from marinade; discarding marinade.

2. Coat a cold cooking grate with cooking spray, and place on grill. Preheat grill to 350° to 400° (medium-high) heat.

3. Grill pork, covered with grill lid, 6 minutes on each side or until a meat thermometer inserted into thickest portion of each chop registers 145°. At the same time, grill onion slices, covered with grill lid, 5 minutes on each side or until crisp-tender; grill peaches, covered with grill lid, 2 minutes on each side or until tender.

4. Remove pork from grill; let stand 5 minutes. Meanwhile, remove and discard peach skins; chop peaches and onion. Stir together peaches, onion, reserved 3 Tbsp. marinade, and vinegar. Serve pork chops with grilled peach relish.

Pesto Chicken Grill

MAKES: 4 SERVINGS   **HANDS-ON TIME:** 30 MIN.
TOTAL TIME: 8 HOURS, 30 MIN.

1	cup zesty Italian dressing
4	(8- to 10-oz.) skinned and boned chicken breasts

Cooking spray

½	tsp. table salt
¼	tsp. pepper
1	medium-size yellow bell pepper, halved and seeded
1	medium-size sweet onion, cut into ½-inch-thick slices
½	(7-oz.) container refrigerated pesto sauce (about ½ cup)

Garnish: sliced fresh basil

1. Place dressing and chicken in a large zip-top plastic freezer bag. Seal bag, turning to coat; chill 8 hours or overnight.

2. Coat a cold cooking grate with cooking spray, and place on grill. Preheat grill to 350° to 400° (medium-high) heat. Remove chicken from marinade, discarding marinade. Sprinkle chicken with salt and pepper.

3. Grill chicken 10 to 12 minutes on each side or until done. At the same time, grill bell pepper and onion slices 4 minutes on each side or until tender and grill marks appear.

4. Remove vegetables from grill; coarsely chop, and place in a medium bowl. Add pesto, tossing to coat. Remove chicken from grill. Let stand 5 minutes. Spoon vegetable mixture over chicken.

Grilled Chicken Caprese

MAKES: 8 SERVINGS   **HANDS-ON TIME:** 27 MIN.
TOTAL TIME: 27 MIN.

Try these easy open-faced sandwiches when you can purchase perfect summer-ripe tomatoes at their peak.

Cooking spray
4   cups diced tomato
1   Tbsp. olive oil
1¼   tsp. kosher salt, divided
¾   tsp. freshly ground pepper, divided
2¼   lb. chicken breast cutlets (8 cutlets)

8   (1-inch-thick) diagonally-cut French bread slices
1   (16-oz.) log presliced fresh mozzarella cheese
¼   cup balsamic glaze
Garnish: fresh basil leaves

1. Coat a cold cooking grate with cooking spray, and place on grill. Preheat grill to 350° to 400° (medium-high) heat.

2. Combine tomato, olive oil, ¼ tsp. salt, and ¼ tsp. pepper in a bowl; toss gently.

3. Sprinkle chicken with remaining 1 tsp. salt and remaining ½ tsp. pepper. Coat chicken with cooking spray, and place on cooking grate. Grill chicken, covered with grill lid, 2 to 3 minutes on each side or until done. Remove from grill; keep warm.

4. Coat both sides of bread slices with cooking spray. Grill bread slices 30 to 45 seconds; turn slices over. Top each bread slice with 2 cheese slices. Grill 30 seconds or until bread is toasted.

5. Arrange chicken cutlets evenly over cheese; top each sandwich with ½ cup tomato mixture. Drizzle each sandwich with 1½ tsp. balsamic glaze.

From My Kitchen

Balsamic glaze, which is a balsamic vinegar reduction, is made by brands like Gia Russa and Monari Federzoni.

Chipotle-Lime Chicken Drumsticks

MAKES: 4 SERVINGS   **HANDS-ON TIME:** 27 MIN.
TOTAL TIME: 27 MIN.

½   cup thick barbecue sauce
1   tsp. ground chipotle chile
    pepper
½   tsp. lime zest
3   lb. chicken drumsticks
    (12 drumsticks)

2   Tbsp. olive oil
1   tsp. table salt
½   tsp. ground black pepper
Garnish: sliced green onions

1. Preheat grill to 350° to 400° (medium-high) heat. Combine first 3 ingredients in a small bowl.

2. Brush chicken with olive oil; sprinkle with salt and pepper. Grill chicken, covered with grill lid, 20 minutes or until chicken is done, turning and basting with sauce mixture every 5 minutes.

• Note: We tested with Stubb's Original Bar-B-Q sauce.

From My Kitchen

If your family likes things a little less spicy, then substitute regular chili powder or cumin for the chipotle chili pepper.

Spicy Honey-Soy Chicken Thighs

MAKES: 4 servings   **HANDS-ON TIME:** 16 min.
TOTAL TIME: 36 min.

Spicy and sweet at the same time, these are sure to please at dinnertime.

¾   cup honey
½   cup soy sauce
3   Tbsp. rice vinegar
1   Tbsp. Asian Sriracha hot chili
     sauce

2   garlic cloves, minced
8   skinned and boned chicken
     thighs
Cooking spray

1. Combine first 5 ingredients in a small bowl; reserve ¼ cup marinade for later use. Place remaining marinade in a shallow dish or large zip-top plastic freezer bag; add chicken. Cover or seal, and chill at least 20 minutes.

2. Meanwhile, preheat grill to 350° to 400° (medium-high) heat. Remove chicken from marinade, discarding marinade. Coat chicken with cooking spray. Grill, covered with grill lid, 6 minutes on each side or until done, brushing with reserved ¼ cup marinade during last 2 minutes of cooking.

Make It A Meal
Add steamed squash for a tasty side to round out the meal.

Sesame-Lime Chicken Wings

MAKES: 5 SERVINGS   **HANDS-ON TIME:** 29 MIN.
TOTAL TIME: 49 MIN.

Serve these chicken wings with mixed salad greens.

½   cup soy sauce
½   cup fresh lime juice (about 4 limes)
6   Tbsp. dark sesame oil
1   tsp. dried crushed red pepper
3   lb. chicken wings
Cooking spray

1. Combine first 4 ingredients in a bowl; reserve half of mixture for later use. Place remaining marinade in a shallow dish or large zip-top plastic freezer bag; add chicken. Cover or seal, and chill 20 minutes.

2. Meanwhile, coat a cold cooking grate with cooking spray, and place on grill over 350° to 400° (medium-high) heat. Remove chicken from marinade, discarding marinade. Grill, covered with grill lid, 24 minutes, turning every 6 minutes or until done. Baste with reserved marinade during last 6 minutes of cooking.

From My Kitchen

Look for limes that are partly yellow with a subtle fragrance. These will be the juiciest, making it much easier to prepare this recipe.

Grilled Curry Chicken Leg Quarters

MAKES: 4 SERVINGS   **HANDS-ON TIME:** 15 MIN.
TOTAL TIME: 50 MIN.

Serve this Indian-flavored dish over a bed of basmati rice.

Cooking spray

1 (12-oz.) jar hot mango chutney

1 Tbsp. curry powder

4 chicken leg quarters (about 4¼ lb.)

1 cup plain yogurt

2 Tbsp. chopped green onion

¼ tsp. table salt

¼ tsp. curry powder

Garnish: fresh cilantro leaves

1. Coat a cold cooking grate with cooking spray, and place on grill. Preheat grill to 400° to 450° (high) heat. Stir together chutney and 1 Tbsp. curry powder in a small saucepan. Cook over medium heat 2 minutes or until melted.

2. Place chicken on grill. Grill, covered with grill lid, 20 minutes. Brush chicken with curry mixture. Turn chicken over, brush with curry mixture, and grill, covered with grill lid, 15 minutes or until done.

3. Combine yogurt and next 3 ingredients in small bowl. Serve with chicken.

Grilled Teriyaki Shrimp Kabobs

MAKES: 6 SERVINGS **HANDS-ON TIME: 16 MIN.**
TOTAL TIME: 16 MIN.

6	(10-inch) wooden skewers	2	Tbsp. olive oil
1	(6-oz.) package uncooked rice vermicelli	½	tsp. table salt
1½	cups fresh pineapple chunks	½	tsp. freshly ground pepper
1½	lb. peeled and deveined large raw shrimp with tails	⅔	cup triple ginger teriyaki sauce
1	(8-oz.) package sweet mini peppers	¼	cup chopped fresh cilantro

1. Soak skewers in water 30 minutes. Preheat grill to 350° to 400° (medium-high) heat. Cook vermicelli according to package directions. Drain and keep warm.

2. Thread pineapple alternately with shrimp and peppers onto each skewer. Brush skewers with olive oil, and sprinkle with salt and pepper.

3. Reserve ⅓ cup teriyaki sauce for serving. Grill kabobs, covered with grill lid, 3 to 4 minutes on each side or just until shrimp turn pink, basting with remaining ⅓ cup teriyaki sauce during last 2 minutes of cooking. Discard basting sauce. Sprinkle kabobs with cilantro. Serve kabobs over vermicelli with reserved ⅓ cup teriyaki sauce.

Mango Thai Grilled Shrimp

MAKES: 4 servings   **HANDS-ON TIME:** 17 min.
TOTAL TIME: 17 min.

3   Tbsp. sweet chili sauce

2   Tbsp. refrigerated ginger
     paste

1   large mango, peeled and
     coarsely chopped

2   lb. large raw shrimp, peeled
     and deveined

4   (12-inch) metal skewers

Fresh cilantro leaves

1. Preheat grill to 350° to 400° (medium-high) heat. Pulse first 3
ingredients in a food processor 6 times or until smooth. Toss shrimp
with half of mango puree, reserving remaining half of puree for later
use. Thread shrimp evenly onto skewers.

2. Grill kabobs, covered with grill lid, 5 minutes on each side or just
until shrimp turn pink. Remove kabobs from grill, and sprinkle with
cilantro. Serve with reserved mango puree.

Asian Calamari and Citrus Salad

MAKES: 4 SERVINGS   **HANDS-ON TIME:** 13 MIN.
TOTAL TIME: 2 HOURS, 13 MIN.

Red curry paste gives this marinated calamari a huge flavor boost. This dish is great hot off the grill or chilled.

3 navel oranges	1 (1-lb.) package cleaned
¼ cup olive oil	calamari (tubes and
¼ cup red curry	tentacles), rinsed
paste	Cooking spray
¼ tsp. table salt	1 cup thinly sliced red onion
¼ tsp. pepper	Fresh cilantro leaves

From My Kitchen

Shrimp can be substitued for the calamari, if you prefer.

1. Grate zest and squeeze juice from 1 orange to equal 1 tsp. and ⅓ cup, respectively. Peel and section remaining 2 oranges. Coarsely chop sections.

2. Whisk together orange zest, orange juice, olive oil, red curry paste, salt, and pepper in a bowl; reserve 3 Tbsp. mixture for later use. Pour remaining marinade into a large shallow dish or zip-top plastic freezer bag; add calamari. Cover or seal, and chill 2 hours, turning occasionally. Remove calamari from marinade, discarding marinade.

3. Coat a cold cooking grate with cooking spray, and place on grill. Preheat grill to 400° to 450° (high) heat. Grill calamari tubes and tentacles, without grill lid, 4 minutes or until firm, turning once.

4. Place calamari in a large bowl; add red onion, cilantro, chopped orange sections, and reserved 3 Tbsp. marinade; toss gently.

Citrus Tilapia and Veggie Pockets

MAKES: 4 SERVINGS
TOTAL TIME: 18 MIN.
HANDS-ON TIME: 18 MIN.

Fish and vegetables all in one flavorful pouch make this delicious meal extra easy.

Heavy-duty aluminum foil
Cooking spray
2 cups thinly sliced zucchini
1 cup thin sweet onion strips
4 garlic cloves, sliced
4 (6-oz.) tilapia fillets

1 tsp. table salt
½ tsp. freshly ground pepper
1 lemon, cut into 4 slices
¼ cup butter, cut into 4 pieces
8 fresh thyme sprigs

1. Preheat grill to 350° to 400° (medium-high) heat. Coat 4 (24- x 15-inch) pieces heavy-duty aluminum foil with cooking spray. Layer ½ cup zucchini and ¼ cup onion strips in center of each. Top evenly with garlic and fish, sprinkling each fillet with ¼ tsp. salt and ⅛ tsp. pepper. Squeeze 1 lemon slice over each fillet. Place lemon slice on top of fish, and top evenly with butter and thyme sprigs. Fold foil to seal.

2. Grill packets, covered with grill lid, 10 minutes or until fish flakes with a fork.

Grilled Mahi-Mahi with Olive Oil and Lemon

MAKES: 4 servings

HANDS-ON TIME: 4 min.

TOTAL TIME: 17 min.

Cooking spray

4   (6-oz.) mahi-mahi fillets
     (1¾ inches thick)

¾   tsp. table salt

¼   tsp. freshly ground pepper

¼   cup lemon juice, divided

3   Tbsp. olive oil, divided

1½   tsp. chopped fresh thyme

4   garlic cloves, minced

1   lemon, sliced

1. Coat a cold cooking grate of grill with cooking spray, and place on grill. Preheat grill to 350° to 400° (medium-high) heat.

2. Sprinkle fish evenly with salt and pepper. Stir together 2 Tbsp. lemon juice, 2 Tbsp. olive oil, thyme, and garlic in a small bowl; brush evenly over fish.

3. Grill fish, covered with grill lid, 5 to 7 minutes on each side or until fish flakes with a fork. Remove fish from grill; drizzle with remaining 2 Tbsp. lemon juice and 1 Tbsp. olive oil. Serve with lemon slices.

Make It A Meal

Serve these lemony fish fillets with baked potatoes and mixed greens to round out your meal.

Grilled Tuna Steaks with Charred Tomato Relish

MAKES: 4 SERVINGS   **HANDS-ON TIME:** 19 MIN.
TOTAL TIME: 19 MIN.

The tomato relish would also work well with any mild white fish or chicken. Add fresh asparagus spears to the grill to serve alongside this grilled main dish.

Cooking spray

1 (10-oz.) package mini San Marzano tomatoes

2 (12-inch) metal skewers

4 (6-oz.) tuna steaks

2 (¼-inch-thick) red onion slices

2 Tbsp. olive oil

½ tsp. table salt, divided

½ tsp. freshly ground pepper, divided

2 Tbsp. chopped fresh flat-leaf parsley

1 Tbsp. red wine vinegar

1. Coat a cold cooking grate with cooking spray, and place on grill. Preheat grill to 400° to 450° (medium-high) heat.

2. Thread tomatoes onto 2 (12-inch) metal skewers. Brush fish, onion, and tomatoes with oil. Sprinkle fish with ¼ tsp. salt and ¼ tsp. pepper.

3. Grill onion, covered with grill lid, 5 minutes on each side or until tender. At the same time, grill fish 2 to 3 minutes on each side or to desired degree of doneness. Grill tomatoes 2 to 3 minutes on each side or until grill marks appear.

4. Chop onion and tomatoes. Toss together vegetables, parsley, vinegar, remaining ¼ tsp. salt, and remaining ¼ tsp. pepper in a medium bowl. Serve over fish.

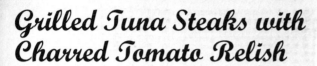

From My Kitchen

Use a mixture of red and yellow grape tomatoes for extra color. Parsley adds a hint of green.

Grilled Salmon with Orange-Fennel Salad

MAKES: 4 SERVINGS   **HANDS-ON TIME:** 17 MIN.
TOTAL TIME: 17 MIN.

This healthy meal is full of bright, fresh flavors and interesting texture combinations.

Cooking spray	4 (6-oz.) salmon fillets
3 navel oranges	(1½ inches thick)
1 fennel bulb	4 tsp. Caribbean seasoning
2 Tbsp. olive oil	⅓ cup orange marmalade
1 tsp. table salt	Garnish: fresh dill
½ tsp. freshly ground pepper	

1. Coat a cold cooking grate with cooking spray, and place on grill. Preheat grill to 350° to 400° (medium-high) heat.

2. Meanwhile, peel oranges and cut crosswise into ¼-inch-thick slices. Rinse fennel thoroughly. Trim and discard root end of fennel bulb. Trim stalks from bulb; chop fronds to measure 2 Tbsp. Set aside for later use. Reserve remaining fronds for another use. Cut bulb lengthwise into quarters; cut quarters crosswise into very thin strips.

3. Place orange slices, fennel strips, olive oil, salt, and pepper in a bowl; toss gently to coat. Cover and chill while preparing salmon.

4. Sprinkle both sides of salmon with Caribbean seasoning; coat with cooking spray. Place salmon, skin side up, on cooking grate. Grill, covered with grill lid, 2 to 3 minutes. Turn salmon over; brush with marmalade. Grill, covered, 2 to 3 minutes or to desired degree of doneness.

5. Place 1 cup orange-fennel salad on each of 4 plates. Top each serving with 1 salmon fillet; sprinkle fillets evenly with 2 Tbsp. reserved fennel fronds.

Make It A Meal

Add some French bread to make this a quick and tasty one-dish meal.

Grilled Vegetables

MAKES: 4 SERVINGS   **HANDS-ON TIME: 15 MIN.**
TOTAL TIME: 35 MIN.

The sugar in the molasses helps carmelize the vegetables, adding a nice hint of sweetness.

1 medium-size red bell pepper, halved and seeded	1 medium-size sweet onion, cut into (½-inch-thick) slices
1 medium-size yellow squash, cut lengthwise into (¼-inch-thick) slices	1 Tbsp. olive oil
	1 Tbsp. molasses
	1 Tbsp. cider vinegar
1 small zucchini, cut lengthwise into (¼-inch-thick) slices	¼ tsp. table salt
	⅛ tsp. freshly ground pepper
	Garnish: fresh parsley

1. Cut bell pepper halves into 1-inch-wide strips. Place bell pepper strips, squash and zucchini slices, and onion in a large bowl. Stir together olive oil, molasses, and vinegar in a small bowl; pour over vegetables, tossing to coat. Sprinkle vegetables with salt and pepper. Cover and let stand at room temperature 20 minutes.

2. Meanwhile, preheat grill to 350° to 400° (medium-high) heat. Remove vegetables from marinade with a slotted spoon, reserving marinade in bowl. Grill vegetables, covered with grill lid, 4 minutes on each side or until tender. Remove vegetables from grill, and return to reserved marinade, tossing to coat. Serve immediately.

Budget Special
Use in-season veggies from the farmers' market in this recipe to take advantage nature's bounty!

Grilled Potato Salad

MAKES: 4 to 6 servings   HANDS-ON TIME: 30 min.
TOTAL TIME: 40 min.

2	lb. medium Yukon gold potatoes, halved	3	garlic cloves, sliced
1	Tbsp. olive oil	½	cup bottled balsamic vinaigrette
¼	tsp. table salt	5	oz. blue cheese, crumbled
¼	tsp. pepper	2	Tbsp. chopped fresh flat-leaf parsley

Heavy-duty aluminum foil

Cooking spray

Garnish: sliced green onions

1. Preheat grill to 350° to 400° (medium-high) heat. Toss potatoes with olive oil in a bowl; sprinkle with salt and pepper.

2. Place potato mixture in a single layer on a 20- x 12-inch piece of heavy-duty aluminum foil coated with cooking spray: sprinkle with garlic slices. Fold foil to seal. Grill 30 minutes, turning foil packet over after 15 minutes.

3. Remove foil packet from grill. Carefully open foil, using tongs. Cool 5 minutes. Place potatoes, vinaigrette, blue cheese, and parsley in a bowl; toss gently to coat.

Sweet Potato and Fennel Salad

MAKES: 7 servings   **HANDS-ON TIME: 30 min.**
TOTAL TIME: 35 min.

Grilling brings out the natural sweetness of the vegetables featured in this colorful salad. Serve warm or at room temperature.

Cooking spray
1½ lb. sweet potatoes
1   medium-size red onion
1   large fennel bulb
1   small head radicchio, cut
     into wedges
⅓   cup canola oil, divided

¾   tsp. table salt, divided
¾   tsp. freshly ground
     pepper, divided
2   Tbsp. white balsamic
     vinegar
1   tsp. sugar
Garnish: fresh thyme sprigs

1. Coat a cold cooking grate with cooking spray, and place on grill. Preheat grill to 350° to 400° (medium-high) heat. Pierce sweet potatoes several times with a fork. Place on a microwave-safe plate; cover with damp paper towels. Microwave at HIGH 5 minutes or until slightly tender. Let stand 5 minutes. Peel and cut in half lengthwise. Cut into long wedges.

2. Peel onion, leaving root end intact. Cut onion vertically into 8 wedges.

3. Rinse fennel thoroughly. Trim and discard root end of fennel bulb. Trim stalks from bulb, reserving fronds for another use. Cut bulb vertically into ⅓-inch slices.

4. Place vegetables on a jelly-roll pan; drizzle with 3 Tbsp. oil. Sprinkle vegetables evenly with ½ tsp. salt and ½ tsp. pepper.

5. Grill fennel, covered with grill lid, 7 minutes on each side or until tender. At the same time, grill onion wedges 5 minutes on each side or until crisp-tender, and grill sweet potatoes 2 minutes on each side. Grill radicchio, without grill lid, 3 minutes on each side or just until wilted. Cut vegetables into 1-inch pieces, discarding root ends of onion and any pieces of core from radicchio. Place vegetables in a large bowl.

6. Combine vinegar, sugar, remaining oil, remaining ¼ tsp. salt, and remaining ¼ tsp. pepper in a small bowl, whisking until sugar dissolves. Drizzle vinaigrette over vegetables, and toss gently to coat.

From My Kitchen

Omit the radicchio and stir in 5 slices cooked, crumbled bacon for a kid-friendly dish.

Grilled Squash and Salsa Verde

MAKES: 4 TO 6 SERVINGS **HANDS-ON TIME: 20 MIN.**
TOTAL TIME: 20 MIN.

4	or 5 assorted medium squash (about 3½ lb.)	1	cup roasted, salted shelled pepitas (pumpkin seeds), toasted
3	Tbsp. olive oil	1	cup salsa verde
¼	tsp. kosher salt	¼	cup crumbled goat cheese

1. Preheat grill to 300° to 350° (medium) heat. Cut squash lengthwise into ¼-inch-thick slices. Toss with olive oil and salt. Grill 10 minutes or until lightly caramelized.

2. Place squash on a serving platter. Top with pepitas, salsa, and goat cheese.

No-Cook Suppers

Serve up fresh, hearty
meals that need no
grill, oven, or stove-top.

Roast Beef and Tomato Jam Wraps

MAKES: 4 SERVINGS
TOTAL TIME: 8 MIN.
HANDS-ON TIME: 8 MIN.

¼	cup mayonnaise	1	lb. thinly sliced deli roast beef
¼	cup tomato chutney		
4	(9-inch) whole wheat wraps	8	(1-oz.) Havarti cheese slices
		2	cups firmly packed arugula

1. Combine mayonnaise and tomato chutney in a small bowl; spread 2 Tbsp. mixture on 1 side of each wrap. Top with roast beef and remaining ingredients; roll up tightly. Cut in half.

• **Note:** We tested with Baxters Tomato Chutney.

Make It A Meal
Serve with crispy French fries. You can also stir 2 Tbsp. prepared horseradish into ½ cup mayonnaise. Spread on one side of wraps in addition to the tomato jam.

Citrus Chicken and Beet Salad

MAKES: 4 SERVINGS **HANDS-ON TIME:** 23 MIN.
TOTAL TIME: 23 MIN.

The convenience of deli-roasted chicken and canned or pickled beets makes this salad a good choice for a weeknight supper.

4	oranges, divided
2	Tbsp. sugar
2	Tbsp. white wine vinegar
½	tsp. table salt
¼	tsp. ground pepper
¼	cup canola oil
6	cups spring greens mix

2	cups shredded deli-roasted chicken breast
1	(15-oz.) can small whole beets, drained and quartered
⅓	cup honey-roasted sliced almonds

1. Grate zest from 1 orange to equal 1 tsp. Cut orange in half; squeeze juice from orange into a measuring cup to equal ⅓ cup. Peel remaining 3 oranges, and cut crosswise into ¼-inch-thick slices.

2. Whisk together orange zest, orange juice, sugar, and next 3 ingredients in a small bowl. Whisk in oil.

3. Toss together spring greens, chicken, beets, and orange slices; arrange on a serving platter. Whisk dressing, and drizzle over salad. Sprinkle with almonds.

• Note: We tested with Almond Accents Honey Roasted Flavored Sliced Almonds.

From My Kitchen
Use vacuum-packed steamed beets instead of canned or pickled beets.

Prosciutto and Tomato Sandwiches

MAKES: 4 SERVINGS **HANDS-ON TIME:** 11 MIN.
TOTAL TIME: 11 MIN.

If blue cheese is too pungent for your taste, use goat cheese or green onion whipped cream cheese in the mayonnaise spread.

⅓ cup mayonnaise

¼ cup crumbled blue cheese

8 (1-oz.) Italian sandwich bread slices

2 cups loosely packed arugula

1 (4-oz.) package thinly sliced prosciutto*

1 large heirloom tomato, sliced

Freshly ground black pepper

1. Stir together mayonnaise and blue cheese in a small bowl. Spread mayonnaise mixture over 1 side of 4 bread slices. Layer 4 bread slices, mayonnaise sides up, evenly with arugula, prosciutto, tomato slices, and pepper. Top with remaining 4 bread slices, mayonnaise sides down.

*Thinly-sliced country ham or bacon may be substituted.

From My Kitchen
Use fresh heirloom tomatoes from your local farmers' market during the summer. Buy presliced fresh Italian bread in the deli of your local grocery store.

Chicken and Black Bean Tostadas

MAKES: 6 SERVINGS **HANDS-ON TIME:** 15 MIN.
TOTAL TIME: 15 MIN.

Dress up these tostadas with additional toppings such as crumbled queso fresco, shredded lettuce, sliced radishes, and pico de gallo.

1	(15-oz.) can refried black beans
6	tostada shells
2	cups shredded mojo-flavored deli-roasted chicken
½	cup refrigerated creamy chipotle ranch dressing
¼	cup chopped fresh cilantro

1. Spread beans over tostada shells; top with chicken. Drizzle with dressing; sprinkle with cilantro. Serve immediately.

Budget Special

Buy whole chickens and romaine lettuce at a "superstore," and incorporate them into your weekly menu planning. Roast a couple of chickens on Sunday to use in your weekday meals.

Curried Mango Chicken Salad

MAKES: 4 SERVINGS **HANDS-ON TIME:** 8 MIN.
TOTAL TIME: 8 MIN.

This tropical-inspired chicken salad gets a kick from curry powder. For a spicier version, try hot Madras curry, or stir in some hot mango chutney.

4	cups chopped deli-roasted chicken	1½	tsp. curry powder
½	cup chopped salted cashews	2	tsp. rice vinegar
1	large mango, peeled and chopped	½	tsp. table salt
1	cup mayonnaise	½	tsp. pepper
		1	head romaine lettuce, shredded
			Garnish: chopped cashews

1. Place first 3 ingredients in a large bowl.

2. Whisk together mayonnaise and next 4 ingredients; add to chicken mixture, stirring gently. Serve over lettuce.

From My Kitchen

Look for mangoes that have more orange or red coloring. Ripe mangoes can be stored in the refrigerator for up to 1 week.

Lemony Chickpea and Chicken Salad

MAKES: 4 SERVINGS   **HANDS-ON TIME:** 5 MIN.
TOTAL TIME: 20 MIN.

Try this dish for a light, refreshing dinner, and take the leftovers to work for lunch.

3 Tbsp. olive oil	2 cups shredded deli-roasted chicken
1 lemon for 1 tsp. zest and 3 Tbsp. juice	1 cup sliced English cucumber
1 Tbsp. Dijon mustard	⅓ cup chopped fresh parsley
½ tsp. table salt	1 (16-oz.) can chickpeas, drained and rinsed
¼ tsp. freshly ground black pepper	

1. Whisk together olive oil, lemon juice, and next 3 ingredients in a large bowl. Add chicken and remaining ingredients, tossing to coat. Top with zest. Cover and chill 15 minutes.

Budget Special

Canned beans are very economical. If you don't have chickpeas in your pantry, use white beans or navy beans instead.

Thai Peanut Chicken Salad

MAKES: 6 SERVINGS **HANDS-ON TIME: 9 MIN.**
TOTAL TIME: 9 MIN.

Most supermarkets offer a selection of peanut sauces in their ethnic food aisle. We tested with House of Tsang Peanut Sauce, which adds a spicy element.

6 oz. fresh snow peas	4 cups shredded deli-roasted chicken
¾ cup peanut sauce	
1½ Tbsp. rice vinegar	½ cup chopped lightly salted peanuts
6 cups shredded broccoli slaw	

1. Trim ends, and remove strings from snow peas; discard ends and strings. Cut peas crosswise into 1-inch pieces.

2. Whisk together peanut sauce, vinegar, and 3 Tbsp. water in a large bowl. Add snow peas, broccoli slaw, and chicken; toss to coat. Stir in peanuts, and serve immediately.

From My Kitchen

To make it gourmet, toss salad ingredients with ½ cup chopped fresh cilantro and ¼ to ⅓ cup chopped green onions, and substitute shredded napa cabbage for the broccoli slaw.

Barbecue Chicken Sandwiches

MAKES: 4 SERVINGS   **HANDS-ON TIME: 8 MIN.**
TOTAL TIME: 8 MIN.

Pick up a warm deli-roasted chicken on the way home from work to toss with your favorite barbecue sauce. If you have chilled chicken on hand, microwave at HIGH 1 minute before tossing with sauce. Choose a barbecue sauce that isn't too sweet for the best flavor combination. We like Stubb's Original Bar-B-Q Sauce.

2 cups shredded deli-roasted chicken	2 cups shredded coleslaw mix
½ cup bottled barbecue sauce	½ cup refrigerated blue cheese dressing
	4 hamburger buns

1. Stir together chicken and barbecue sauce. Stir together coleslaw mix and blue cheese dressing. Spoon ½ cup chicken mixture and ½ cup coleslaw mixture onto each hamburger bun.

From My Kitchen

Use a pan of cornbread cut into squares and halved horizontally instead of the bun for a Southern twist.

Shrimp-Asian Noodle Salad

MAKES: 4 SERVINGS   **HANDS-ON TIME:** 5 MIN.
TOTAL TIME: 15 MIN.

This quick salad relies on the convenience of cellophane noodles (also known as glass noodles or mung bean vermicelli), which are made from ground mung beans. When soaked, the noodles become soft and translucent and provide a perfect foil for flavorful sauces.

1	(3.75-oz.) package bean threads (cellophane noodles)	1½	cups fresh bean sprouts
12	oz. cooked shrimp	½	cup bottled sweet chili sauce
1	(12-oz.) package Asian blend salad greens (reserve dressing for another use)	2	Tbsp. rice wine vinegar
		1	Tbsp. soy sauce

1. Prepare noodles according to package directions, soaking noodles in warm, not boiling, water. Drain. Rinse with cold water, and drain. Snip noodles several times, using kitchen shears. Place noodles, shrimp, and next 2 ingredients in a large bowl.

2. Whisk together sweet chili sauce and remaining ingredients in a bowl; pour over noodle mixture, tossing gently to coat.

Make It A Meal

Serve alongside Asian-style marinated grilled chicken or beef. Sweeten this "perfect for summer" salad by adding thinly sliced ripe mango or papaya.

Shrimp, Corn, and Tomato Salad with Pesto Vinaigrette

MAKES: 4 SERVINGS   **HANDS-ON TIME:** 10 MIN.
TOTAL TIME: 10 MIN.

Most grocery stores and seafood markets will steam shrimp, upon request. Leave off any seasoning so that it won't compete with the pesto.

⅔ cup refrigerated pesto sauce	1 lb. steamed shrimp, peeled and chilled
3 Tbsp. white wine vinegar	
¼ tsp. table salt	1 cup fresh corn kernels (2 ears)
¼ tsp. freshly ground black pepper	1 pint grape tomatoes, halved
	Boston lettuce leaves (optional)

1. Whisk together first 4 ingredients in a medium bowl. Add shrimp, corn, and tomatoes, tossing to coat. Serve over lettuce leaves, if desired.

Asian Shrimp and Noodle Salad

MAKES: 6 SERVINGS **HANDS-ON TIME: 10 MIN.**
TOTAL TIME: 20 MIN.

1 (6-oz.) package rice vermicelli, broken	1 lb. cooked shrimp, peeled and deveined
1 (6-oz.) package fresh snow peas	Garnishes: fresh cilantro leaves, lime wedges, or chopped wasabi almonds
1 cup matchstick-cut carrots	
1 cup low-fat sesame-ginger dressing	

1. Bring 2 qt. water to a boil in a Dutch oven. Stir in vermicelli; cook 2 to 3 minutes or just until softened. Drain and plunge into cold water to stop the cooking process. Let stand in cold water 5 to 8 minutes or until completely cool; drain.

2. Trim ends, and remove strings from snow peas; discard ends, and strings. Combine snow peas, carrots, dressing, and shrimp; toss well.

• Note: We tested with Newman's Own Lite Low Fat Sesame Ginger Dressing.

Budget Special

Feel free to substitute other vegetables, such as broccoli, to use up whatever you have in your fridge.

Crab Salad in Avocado Cups

MAKES: 4 SERVINGS   **HANDS-ON TIME:** 12 MIN.
TOTAL TIME: 12 MIN.

1	lb. fresh lump crabmeat, drained	2	tsp. Dijon mustard
4	avocados	1	green onion, chopped
⅓	cup mayonnaise	¼	tsp. table salt
1½	Tbsp. drained capers, chopped	¼	tsp. freshly ground black pepper
			Garnish: chopped parsley

1. Pick crabmeat, removing any bits of shell.

2. Cut avocados in half. Scoop avocado pulp into a bowl, leaving a ¼-inch shell. Reserve shells.

3. Mash avocado with a fork or potato masher just until chunky. Add mayonnaise and next 5 ingredients, stirring until blended; fold in crabmeat. Spoon mixture into avocado shells.

From My Kitchen
Run cut avocados under cold water to prevent browning. Avocados keep well in the refrigerator.

Tuscan Tuna Salad with White Beans

MAKES: 4 SERVINGS   **HANDS-ON TIME:** 8 MIN.
TOTAL TIME: 8 MIN.

3	Tbsp. olive oil	2	(4.5-oz.) cans solid white tuna in spring water, drained and flaked
2½	Tbsp. lemon juice (1 lemon)		
1	Tbsp. chopped fresh parsley		
½	tsp. table salt	1	(15-oz.) can cannellini beans, drained and rinsed
½	tsp. freshly ground pepper		
2	garlic cloves, minced		Fresh baby spinach leaves (optional)
2	plum tomatoes, chopped		

1. Whisk together first 6 ingredients in a large bowl. Add tomato, tuna, and beans, tossing to coat. Serve over spinach leaves, if desired.

Make It A Meal
Serve this protein-packed salad with crusty Italian bread, spooned into pita pockets, or over a bed of fresh baby spinach.

Smoked Salmon Wrap

MAKES: 5 SERVINGS   **HANDS-ON TIME: 11 MIN.**
TOTAL TIME: 11 MIN.

Find hot smoked salmon in the seafood department.

⅔	cup chive and onion cream cheese
1	(14-oz.) package flatbread
2	(4-oz.) packages smoked salmon
½	cup sliced red onion
2	Tbsp. drained capers

1. Spread about 2 Tbsp. cream cheese over each flatbread. Divide salmon, onion, and capers among flatbreads. Fold in half, and secure with wooden picks.

• Note: We tested with Toufayan Hearty White Flatbread.

From My Kitchen

You can also use smoked trout in this wrap. Substitute regular pita bread for flatbread to create pocket sandwiches.

Heirloom Tomato Panzanella

MAKES: 5 SERVINGS **HANDS-ON TIME:** 8 MIN.
TOTAL TIME: 8 MIN.

This simple Italian salad derives its incredible flavor from summer's bounty of ripe, sweet heirloom tomatoes.

⅓	cup light sun-dried tomato vinaigrette	2	lb. heirloom tomatoes, coarsely chopped
2	Tbsp. red wine vinegar	5	cups (I-inch) day-old French bread or other rustic bread cubes
½	tsp. table salt		
½	tsp. freshly ground pepper		Garnish: fresh basil leaves
I	English cucumber		
½	red onion, quartered		

1. Whisk together first 4 ingredients in a large bowl. Cut cucumber into half-moon-shaped slices. Cut onion quarters crosswise into thin strips. Add cucumber, onion, and tomato to dressing mixture, tossing to coat. Add bread cubes just before serving; toss gently.

Make It A Meal
Serve this delicious summer salad with roast chicken from your supermarket deli.

Cornbread-Vegetable Salad

MAKES: 5 SERVINGS **HANDS-ON TIME:** 4 MIN.
TOTAL TIME: 4 MIN.

This is a great use for leftover cornbread or corn muffins. No leftovers? Pick up cornbread in the bakery section, or make your own semi-homemade from a mix.

6 slices precooked bacon, crumbled and divided

3 cups crumbled cornbread

1 cup bottled refrigerated buttermilk Ranch dressing

1 (8-oz.) container prechopped tricolored bell pepper

1½ cups (6-oz.) shredded sharp Cheddar cheese

1. Reserve 2 Tbsp. bacon crumbles. Combine cornbread, next 2 ingredients, 1¼ cups cheese, and remaining bacon crumbles in a medium bowl; toss to coat. Sprinkle with remaining cheese and bacon.

From My Kitchen

Substitute other flavors of Ranch dressing instead of the buttermilk Ranch. You can also substitute pepper Jack cheese for the Cheddar.

Lemon Zucchini Ribbons

MAKES: 5 SERVINGS **HANDS-ON TIME:** 10 MIN.
TOTAL TIME: 1 HOUR, 10 MIN.

Zucchini is thinly sliced with a vegetable peeler to mimic pasta in this brightly flavored side dish. A mandoline could also be used.

1	large lemon	¼	tsp. freshly ground black pepper
2	Tbsp. olive oil		
2	garlic cloves, pressed	⅓	cup torn fresh basil leaves
6	medium-size zucchini	¼	cup chopped salted almonds
½	tsp. table salt		

1. Grate zest from lemon to equal 1 tsp. Cut lemon in half; squeeze juice from lemon into a measuring cup to equal 3 Tbsp. Whisk zest, juice, olive oil, and garlic in a large bowl.

2. Trim ends of zucchini. Using a vegetable peeler, peel zucchini lengthwise into long, thin ribbons. Add zucchini ribbons, salt and pepper to lemon juice mixture; toss to combine. Refrigerate 1 hour. Sprinkle with basil and almonds before serving.

Gazpacho

MAKES: 8 servings   **HANDS-ON TIME:** 8 min.
TOTAL TIME: 1 hour, 8 min.

Look for pico de gallo in the produce section at your local supermarket, and choose mild or hot depending on your taste.

- 4 cups spicy tomato juice, chilled and divided
- 1 English cucumber, chopped and divided
- ½ cup loosely packed fresh cilantro leaves
- 1 (12-oz.) jar roasted red bell peppers, drained
- 1 (8-oz.) container refrigerated pico de gallo or chunky salsa
- ¼ tsp. table salt
- ¼ tsp. freshly ground black pepper

Garnishes: cilantro leaves, chopped cucumber

1. Process 2 cups tomato juice, half of chopped cucumber and next 5 ingredients in a blender until smooth. Pour mixture into a large bowl; stir in remaining 2 cups tomato juice and remaining chopped cucumber. Cover and chill 1 hour.

Pastas
and Pizzas

Serve these classic yet quick
one-dish favorites for
a tasty weeknight meal.

Philly Cheesesteak Pizza

MAKES: 4 SERVINGS   **HANDS-ON TIME:** 13 MIN.
TOTAL TIME: 31 MIN.

Precooked beef roast makes this pizza a quick and easy fix. You can find it with the lunchmeat in your local grocery store.

1 lb. bakery pizza dough, at room temperature	1 Tbsp. olive oil
Parchment paper	1 (17-oz.) package fully cooked beef roast au jus
1 (14-oz.) package frozen pepper and onion stir-fry vegetables, thawed	8 oz. sharp provolone cheese, shredded

1. Preheat oven to 450°. Stretch dough into a 12-inch circle on 17- x 12-inch parchment paper-lined half baking sheet.

2. Sauté vegetables in hot oil in a large nonstick skillet over medium-high heat 5 minutes or until tender.

3. Heat beef according to package directions. Shred beef in juices in container using 2 forks. Remove beef with a slotted spoon. Top pizza dough with beef and sautéed vegetables. Sprinkle with cheese.

4. Bake at 450° for 18 minutes or until crust is golden.

From My Kitchen
To make the dough easier to stretch, let it rest 5 minutes before working with it.

Barbecue Pork Pizza

**MAKES: 3 TO 4 SERVINGS   HANDS-ON TIME: 8 MIN.
TOTAL TIME: 26 MIN.**

1 lb. bakery pizza dough, at room temperature	½ cup spicy barbecue sauce
Parchment paper	¾ lb. shredded barbecued pork without sauce, warmed
1½ cups vertically sliced red onion	
1 Tbsp. olive oil	1½ cups (6 oz.) shredded Monterey Jack cheese

1. Preheat oven to 450°. Roll pizza dough into a 12-inch circle on a parchment paper-lined baking sheet.

2. Sauté onion in hot oil in a large nonstick skillet over medium-high heat 5 minutes or until tender.

3. Combine barbecue sauce and pork. Top dough with pork mixture and onion. Sprinkle with cheese.

4. Bake at 450° for 18 minutes or until crust is golden.

From My Kitchen

Line a baking sheet with parchment paper to make cleanup even easier.

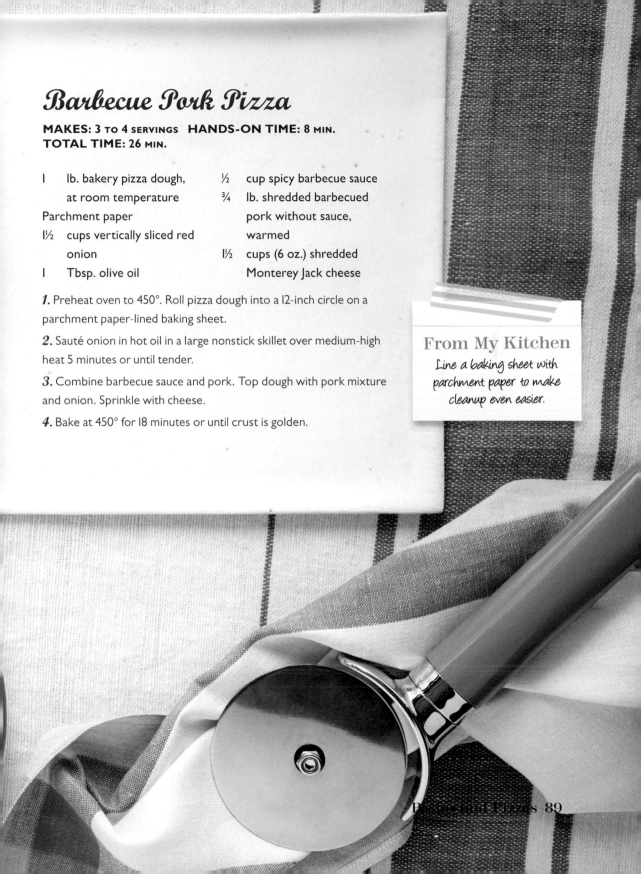

Brussels Sprouts, Bacon, and Italian Cheese Pizza

MAKES: 4 servings   **HANDS-ON TIME:** 15 min.
TOTAL TIME: 30 min.

This pizza is a surefire way to bring your kids around to the virtues of Brussels sprouts. Even those with picky palates are likely to clean their plates.

½   lb. fresh Brussels sprouts
1   lb. bakery pizza dough, at room temperature
Cooking spray
2   Tbsp. olive oil, divided
1   (8-oz.) package shredded Italian three-cheese blend, divided

1   lemon
8   slices bacon, cooked and crumbled
½   tsp. kosher salt
¼   tsp. freshly ground pepper

1. Preheat oven to 450°. Cut Brussels sprouts in half, and cut into shreds.

2. Roll dough into a 12-inch circle on a baking sheet coated with cooking spray. Brush dough with 1 Tbsp oil. Sprinkle with 1½ cups cheese, leaving a ½-inch border.

3. Grate zest from lemon to equal 2 tsp. Cut lemon in half; squeeze juice from lemon into a large bowl to equal 1 Tbsp. Add lemon zest, Brussels sprouts, bacon, next 2 ingredients, and remaining 1 Tbsp oil; toss well. Sprinkle Brussels sprouts mixture over pizza. Top with remaining ½ cup cheese.

4. Bake at 450° for 15 minutes or until crust is golden, cheese is bubbly, and edges of sprouts are browned.

From My Kitchen

To assemble this pizza even faster, buy precooked bacon. Shred the Brussels sprouts ahead, and store them in the refrigerator in a zip-top plastic bag.

Sausage-Mushroom Pizza

MAKES: 4 SERVINGS　　**HANDS-ON TIME:** 16 MIN.
TOTAL TIME: 33 MIN.

8	oz. mild Italian pork sausage, casings removed
2	(8-oz.) packages sliced baby portobello mushrooms
½	tsp. table salt
¼	tsp. dried crushed red pepper
1	(16-oz.) package prebaked Italian pizza crust
1	cup pizza sauce
1	(8-oz.) package shredded Italian three-cheese blend
½	tsp. freshly ground black pepper

1. Preheat oven to 400°. Brown sausage in a large nonstick skillet over medium-high heat, stirring often, 6 minutes or until sausage crumbles and is no longer pink; remove sausage, reserving 2 tsp. drippings. Cook mushrooms in hot drippings, stirring often, 10 minutes or until browned and tender. Stir sausage, salt, and crushed red pepper into mushrooms.

2. Place pizza crust on a baking sheet; spread pizza sauce over crust, leaving a ½-inch border. Top evenly with cooked mushroom mixture; sprinkle with cheese and black pepper.

3. Bake at 400° for 12 minutes or until cheese melts and is bubbly.

Make It A Meal

Serve this hearty, meaty pizza with a green salad on the side for a filling meal fit for a crowd.

Chicken, Artichoke, and Sun-Dried Tomato Pizza

MAKES: 4 SERVINGS   **HANDS-ON TIME:** 8 MIN.
TOTAL TIME: 20 MIN.

Serve this hearty pizza with a simple green salad.

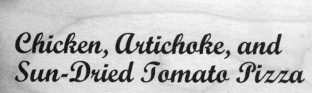

1½	Tbsp. olive oil
1	lb. bakery pizza dough, at room temperature
⅓	cup jarred sun-dried tomato pesto sauce*
2	cups shredded deli-roasted chicken

1	(7.5-oz.) jar marinated quartered artichoke hearts, drained
1	(8-oz.) package shredded Italian three-cheese blend
Garnish: fresh oregano leaves	

1. Preheat oven to 450°. Brush a baking sheet with olive oil. Stretch pizza dough into a 12-inch circle on baking sheet.

2. Spread pesto sauce over dough, leaving a ½-inch border. Top with chicken and artichoke hearts. Sprinkle with cheese.

3. Bake at 450° for 12 minutes or until edges of crust are golden and cheese melts.

*Traditional basil pesto sauce may be substituted.

From My Kitchen
Mix up the flavor by using a different flavor of rotisserie chicken, such as barbecue or mojo.

Creamy Blue, Pancetta, and Fig Pizza

MAKES: 3 TO 4 SERVINGS **HANDS-ON TIME:** 12 MIN.
TOTAL TIME: 32 MIN.

This decadent pizza, made with creamy Cambozola (a combination of triple cream cheese and Gorgonzola), spicy pancetta, and sweet figs, delivers full flavor.

½ cup chopped dried Mission figs

½ lb. sliced pancetta

2 tsp. olive oil

1 lb. bakery pizza dough, at room temperature

½ cup refrigerated Alfredo sauce

6 oz. Cambozola cheese (or other soft ripened blue cheese), rind removed and cut into ½-inch pieces

1. Preheat oven to 450°. Place figs in a 1-cup glass measuring cup; cover with water. Microwave, uncovered, at HIGH 1 minute; let stand 10 minutes or until softened. Drain.

2. Cook pancetta in 2 batches in a large skillet over medium-high heat 2 to 3 minutes or until crisp; remove pancetta, and drain on paper towels. Crumble pancetta.

3. Brush a baking sheet with olive oil. Stretch dough into a 12-inch circle on pan. Bake at 450° for 10 minutes.

4. Spread Alfredo sauce evenly on pizza dough, leaving a ½-inch border. Top with cheese, figs, and pancetta. Bake 10 more minutes or until crust is golden and cheese is bubbly.

• Note: Goat cheese can be substituted for blue cheese.

From My Kitchen

Pancetta is unsmoked pork belly cured in salt and spices. If you can't find it in the deli section of the supermarket, ask the butcher to slice some for you.

White Pizza with Baby Greens

MAKES: 4 SERVINGS   **HANDS-ON TIME:** 10 MIN.
TOTAL TIME: 25 MIN.

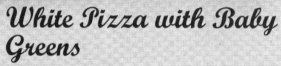

1 lb. bakery pizza dough, at room temperature	½ tsp. kosher salt, divided
Parchment paper	¼ tsp. freshly ground black pepper, divided
½ cup (2 oz.) freshly grated pecorino Romano cheese	1 Tbsp. olive oil
½ (16-oz.) package sliced fresh mozzarella cheese	2 tsp. balsamic vinegar
	4 cups baby greens

1. Preheat oven to 450°. Stretch pizza dough into a 12-inch circle on baking sheet lined with parchment paper. Sprinkle dough with pecorino Romano cheese; top with mozzarella slices. Sprinkle with ¼ tsp. kosher salt and ⅛ tsp. pepper.

2. Bake at 450° for 15 minutes or until crust is thoroughly cooked, edges are golden, and cheese melts.

3. Meanwhile, whisk oil, balsamic vinegar, remaining ¼ tsp. kosher salt, and remaining ⅛ tsp. pepper together in a medium bowl. Add greens; toss to coat. Top pizza with greens.

From My Kitchen

Serve this pizza immediately because the greens will start to wilt soon after they are placed on the hot cheese.

Zucchini, Onion, and Triple-Cheese Pizza

MAKES: 4 SERVINGS **HANDS-ON TIME:** 10 MIN.
TOTAL TIME: 28 MIN.

This light and fresh pizza is perfect for summer nights when you have plenty of zucchini from your garden.

1   lb. bakery pizza dough, room temperature
Parchment paper
½   cup refrigerated pesto with basil
2   cups thinly sliced zucchini
¼   cup thinly sliced sweet onion
½   tsp. garlic salt
1½ cups (6 oz.) shredded Italian three-cheese blend
Garnish: oregano leaves

1. Preheat oven to 425°. Stretch pizza dough into a 12-inch circle on a baking sheet lined with parchment paper. Spread pesto over dough in a thin layer to within ½-inch of edge.

2. Arrange zucchini in overlapping slices over pesto. Sprinkle onion rings over zucchini. Sprinkle with garlic salt, and top with cheese.

3. Bake at 425° for 18 to 20 minutes or until vegetables are lightly browned and cheese is bubbly.

Budget Special
Purchase a large jar of refrigerated pesto. Use half a cup for this recipe, and select another recipe that uses pesto to serve another night of the week.

Apple and Goat Cheese Pizza

MAKES: 6 SERVINGS **HANDS-ON TIME:** 20 MIN.
TOTAL TIME: 40 MIN.

1 (11-oz.) can refrigerated thin pizza crust dough
1 Granny Smith apple, thinly sliced
½ cup thinly sliced red onion
2 tsp. olive oil
⅓ cup fig preserves
4 oz. crumbled goat cheese
Garnish: arugula, chopped toasted pecans

1. Preheat oven to 450°. Unroll dough; pat to an even thickness on a lightly greased baking sheet. Bake 10 to 12 minutes or until lightly browned.

2. Sauté apple and onion in hot oil in a nonstick skillet until tender. Spread fig preserves over crust. Top with apple mixture and goat cheese. Bake at 450° for 8 to 10 minutes or until cheese is slightly melted.

Budget Special
You can substitute whichever apples you have on hand.

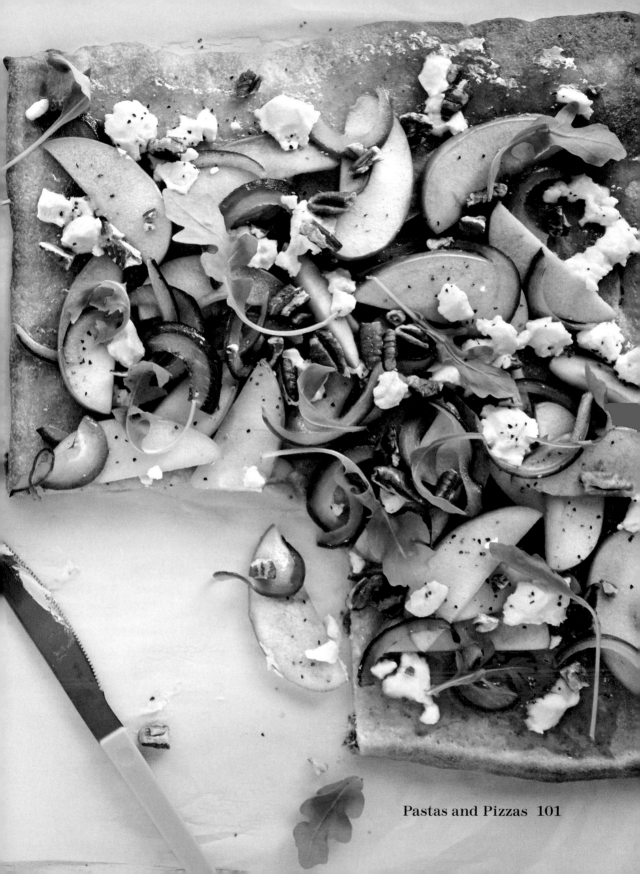

Pecorino, Arugula, and Tomato Pizza

MAKES: 6 servings   **HANDS-ON TIME:** 15 min.
TOTAL TIME: 25 min.

Cooking spray
1 lb. bakery pizza dough,
   at room temperature
6 Tbsp. refrigerated
   Alfredo sauce
4 small plum tomatoes,
   halved

2 cups loosely packed
   baby arugula
2 Tbsp. olive oil
¼ tsp. table salt
¼ tsp. freshly ground
   black pepper
½ cup shaved pecorino
   or Parmesan cheese

1. Coat a cold cooking grate with cooking spray, and place on grill. Preheat grill to 350° (medium).

2. Divide dough into 6 equal portions. Stretch each portion into a 5-inch circle (about ¼-inch thick) on a lightly floured surface. Carefully transfer circles to a baking sheet. Spread 1 Tbsp. Alfredo sauce over each circle.

3. Carefully slide circles onto cooking grate. Grill circles, covered with grill lid, 4 minutes. At the same time, grill tomato halves 3 minutes on each side or until grill marks appear. Rotate each crust one-quarter turn, and grill, covered with grill lid, 5 more minutes or until golden. Remove crusts and tomato halves from grill. Coarsely chop tomato halves.

4. Toss together arugula and next 3 ingredients. Top crusts evenly with tomato, arugula mixture, and cheese. Serve immediately.

From My Kitchen

When looking for tomatoes, select those that are plump, firm, and vibrant in color. When out of season, use canned diced tomatoes, drained and patted dry.

Pastas and Pizzas 103

Grilled Tomato-Peach Pizza

MAKES: 4 SERVINGS   **HANDS-ON TIME:** 26 MIN.
TOTAL TIME: 26 MIN.

Cooking spray
2   tomatoes, sliced
½   tsp. table salt
1   large peach, peeled and
    sliced
1   lb. bakery pizza dough, at
    room temperature

½   (16-oz.) package fresh
    mozzarella, sliced
4 to 6 fresh basil leaves
Garnishes: coarsely ground
      pepper, olive oil

1. Coat cold cooking grate of grill with cooking spray, and place on grill. Preheat grill to 350° (medium).

2. Sprinkle tomatoes with salt; let stand 15 minutes. Pat tomatoes dry with paper towels.

3. Grill peach slices, covered with grill lid, 2 to 3 minutes on each side or until grill marks appear.

4. Place dough on a large baking sheet coated with cooking spray; lightly coat dough with cooking spray. Roll dough to ¼-inch thickness (about 14 inches in diameter). Slide pizza dough from baking sheet onto cooking grate.

5. Grill, covered with grill lid, 2 to 3 minutes or until lightly browned. Turn dough over, and reduce temperature to 250° to 300° (low); top dough with tomatoes, grilled peaches, and mozzarella. Grill, covered with grill lid, 5 minutes or until cheese melts. Arrange basil leaves over pizza. Serve immediately.

Budget Special

Buy a basket of peaches in the summer to use for this tasty pizza. Leftover peaches can be served with ice cream or grilled pound cake.

Wild Mushroom and Butternut Squash Pizza

MAKES: 4 SERVINGS **HANDS-ON TIME:** 20 MIN.
TOTAL TIME: 30 MIN.

This autumn-inspired pizza balances the earthiness of exotic mushrooms with the sweetness of butternut squash.

3	Tbsp. olive oil, divided	1½	tsp. chopped fresh rosemary
1	lb. bakery pizza dough, at room temperature	½	tsp. salt
		¼	tsp. freshly ground pepper
2	(4-oz.) packages gourmet mushroom blend	8	oz. (2 cups) fontina cheese, shredded and divided
½	small butternut squash, peeled and cubed (about 2 cups)		

1. Preheat oven to 450°. Brush a large baking sheet with 1 Tbsp. olive oil. Stretch dough into a 12-inch circle on pan. Bake for 10 minutes.

2. Meanwhile, sauté mushrooms in 1 Tbsp. hot oil in a large skillet over medium-high heat 4 minutes or until liquid evaporates. Transfer to a bowl.

3. In same skillet, sauté butternut squash in remaining 1 Tbsp. hot oil over medium-high heat 3 minutes or until lightly browned. Reduce heat to medium. Stir in rosemary, salt, and pepper; cover and cook 8 minutes or until tender, stirring occasionally.

4. Sprinkle 1½ cups cheese evenly on pizza crust, leaving a ½-inch border. Top with butternut squash and mushrooms. Sprinkle with remaining ½ cup cheese. Bake at 450° for 10 more minutes or until crust is golden and cheese melts.

From My Kitchen

To save some prep time, buy pre-diced butternut squash from the produce section of the supermarket. Goat cheese would also pair well with these flavors.

Beet and Goat Cheese Pizza

MAKES: 4 SERVINGS **HANDS-ON TIME:** 8 MIN.
TOTAL TIME: 28 MIN.

This Mediterranean-inspired pizza combines caramelized
onions, cooked beets, and a blend of cheeses.

1	large onion, vertically sliced	½	cup (2 oz.) shredded Italian three-cheese blend
2	Tbsp. olive oil, divided	1	(4-oz.) package goat cheese with herbs, crumbled
1	lb. bakery pizza dough, at room temperature	½	tsp. kosher salt
1	(10-oz.) package vacuum-packed precooked beets, thinly sliced	¼	tsp. freshly ground black pepper
			Garnish: thyme leaves

1. Preheat oven to 450°. Sauté onion in 1 Tbsp. hot oil in a large
nonstick skillet over medium-high heat 10 to 15 minutes or until
tender and caramel colored.

2. Brush a baking sheet with remaining 1 Tbsp. oil. Stretch dough
into a 12-inch circle on pan. Arrange onion evenly on pizza dough,
leaving a ½-inch border. Top with beets and cheeses. Sprinkle with
salt and pepper. Bake at 450° for 20 minutes or until crust is golden.

From My Kitchen

*Use Love Beets for the
vacuum-packed precooked
beets, which are available
in the produce section of
your supermarket.*

Chicken-Prosciutto Primavera Pasta

MAKES: 4 SERVINGS   **HANDS-ON TIME:** 12 MIN.
TOTAL TIME: 12 MIN.

Fresh asparagus and spring vegetables, chicken and prosciutto-filled tortelloni, and creamy Alfredo sauce combine in this delicious and satisfying dish.

2   (9-oz.) packages refrigerated chicken and prosciutto tortelloni or other refrigerated tortelloni
½   lb. fresh asparagus, cut into 1-inch pieces
1   cup matchstick carrots

1   cup frozen baby sweet peas
1   (15-oz.) jar Alfredo sauce
½   tsp. freshly ground black pepper
¼   tsp. table salt

1. Cook pasta according to package directions, omitting salt and oil, and adding asparagus, carrots, and peas to boiling water during last 2 minutes of cooking; drain. Return pasta and vegetables to pan.

3. Stir in Alfredo sauce, tossing to coat. Sprinkle with pepper and salt. Serve immediately.

• Note: We tested with Buitoni Chicken & Prosciutto Tortelloni and Bertolli Alfredo Sauce.

Budget Special
Look for large packages of fresh filled pastas at your local superstore, and freeze the unused portion for another meal.

Kielbasa and Mini Pierogi Sauté

MAKES: 4 SERVINGS   **HANDS-ON TIME:** 17 MIN.
TOTAL TIME: 17 MIN.

A crisp salad can finish out the meal.

- 1 (16-oz.) package potato and onion mini pierogies
- 1 tsp. canola oil
- 1 (14-oz.) package kielbasa, cut into ¼-inch-thick slices
- 1 (14-oz.) package frozen pepper and onion stir-fry vegetables, thawed
- ¾ cup hard cider or apple juice
- 1½ Tbsp. Dijon mustard
- Garnish: chopped fresh thyme, dried crushed red pepper

1. Prepare pierogies according to package directions; keep warm.

2. Meanwhile, heat oil in a large nonstick skillet over medium-high heat. Add kielbasa and vegetables; sauté 7 minutes or until kielbasa is lightly browned and vegetables are tender. Add cider; reduce heat to medium, and cook, uncovered, 1 minute. Stir in mustard; cook 2 minutes, stirring occasionally. Add pierogies; cook 2 minutes. Serve immediately.

• Note: We tested with Rising Moon Organics Pierogies and Woodchuck Amber hard cider.

From My Kitchen
Use apple juice in place of hard cider for a kid-friendly version.

Pasta Vodka with Roasted Red Peppers

MAKES: 8 SERVINGS   **HANDS-ON TIME:** 21 MIN.
TOTAL TIME: 21 MIN.

Using jarred roasted bell peppers not only saves you time in the kitchen, but it also adds a smoky flavor to any dish.

1	lb. uncooked penne or ziti pasta
1	(12-oz.) jar roasted red bell peppers, drained and chopped
2	Tbsp. olive oil
½	cup vodka

1	(24-oz.) jar hot Sicilian-style pasta sauce
⅔	cup whipping cream
½	tsp. table salt

Garnishes: freshly grated Parmesan cheese, chopped fresh Italian parsley

1. Cook pasta according to package directions; drain.

2. Meanwhile, cook peppers in hot oil in a large nonstick skillet over medium-high heat 4 minutes. Remove from heat; stir in vodka. Bring to a simmer over medium heat; cook 4 minutes. Stir in pasta sauce, and simmer 5 minutes. Stir in cream and salt; simmer, stirring occasionally, 3 minutes. Stir in pasta. Serve immediately.

• Note: We tested with Gia Russa Hot Sicilian pasta sauce.

Fresh Tomato-Spinach Pasta

MAKES: 8 servings **HANDS-ON TIME:** 20 min.
TOTAL TIME: 20 min.

- 1 (16-oz.) package penne pasta
- 1 large sweet onion, chopped
- 3 Tbsp. olive oil
- 4 large tomatoes (about 3½ lb.), chopped
- 3 garlic cloves, minced
- 1 (6-oz.) package baby spinach
- 2 Tbsp. butter
- 1 tsp. table salt
- ½ tsp. freshly ground black pepper

Garnish: freshly grated Parmesan cheese

1. Cook pasta according to package directions; drain and keep warm.

2. Meanwhile, sauté onion in hot oil in a large nonstick skillet over medium-high heat until tender. Add tomato and garlic. Cook, stirring often, 4 minutes. Add spinach; cook, stirring constantly, 2 minutes or until all of the spinach has wilted. Add butter, salt, and pepper, stirring until butter melts. Serve immediately over hot cooked pasta.

From My Kitchen

Use baby spinach in this dish; it's sweeter and more tender than regular spinach.

Creamy Bacon and Leek Pasta

MAKES: 4 SERVINGS   **HANDS-ON TIME: 26 MIN.**
TOTAL TIME: 26 MIN.

This quick-and-easy pasta dish is sure to be a crowd-pleaser.

12 oz. uncooked fusili pasta	¾ cup freshly grated Parmesan cheese, divided
2 leeks	
6 hickory-smoked bacon slices	¼ tsp. table salt
2 cups whipping cream	¼ tsp. freshly ground black pepper

1. Cook pasta according to package directions; drain.

2. Meanwhile, remove and discard root ends and dark green tops of leeks. Cut in half lengthwise, and rinse thoroughly under cold running water to remove grit and sand. Thinly slice leeks.

3. Cook bacon in a large skillet over medium-high heat 6 minutes or until crisp; remove bacon, and drain on paper towels, reserving 2 Tbsp. drippings in skillet. Crumble bacon.

4. Sauté leeks in hot drippings 4 minutes or until tender; stir in cream. Bring to a boil; reduce heat, and simmer, uncovered, 7 minutes or until thickened.

5. Stir in pasta, crumbled bacon, ½ cup Parmesan cheese, salt, and pepper. Cook 1 minute or until cheese melts. Sprinkle with remaining Parmesan cheese. Serve immediately.

Make It A Meal
Serve with mixed greens drizzled with balsamic vinegar and olive oil or sautéed broccoli. Add crusty French bread.

Spaghetti with Mushroom-White Bean Ragout

MAKES: 6 servings   **HANDS-ON TIME:** 19 min.
TOTAL TIME: 29 min.

This hearty sauce is a great option for a meatless dinner.

- 1 (16 oz.) package uncooked spaghetti
- 4 garlic cloves, minced
- 1 medium onion, chopped
- 3 Tbsp. olive oil
- 1 (8-oz.) package sliced baby portobello mushrooms
- ½ tsp. table salt
- ½ tsp. freshly ground black pepper
- 2 (14.5-oz.) cans diced tomatoes with basil, garlic, and oregano, undrained
- 1 (15.5-oz.) can cannellini beans, drained and rinsed

Garnish: parsly leaves

1. Cook pasta according to package directions; drain and keep warm.

2. Meanwhile, sauté garlic and onion in hot oil in a large skillet over medium-high heat 4 minutes or until tender. Stir in mushrooms, and cook, stirring occasionally, 5 minutes, or just until tender. Stir in salt and remaining ingredients. Bring to a boil, reduce heat, and simmer, uncovered, 5 minutes or until slightly thickened. Serve sauce over pasta.

From My Kitchen

Use a large pot and plenty of water for best results when cooking pasta.

Tomato, Roasted Garlic, and Mushroom Pasta

MAKES: 8 SERVINGS   **HANDS-ON TIME:** 17 MIN.
TOTAL TIME: 17 MIN.

This easy weeknight pasta is earthy and satisfying.

- 12 oz. uncooked penne pasta
- 2 (8-oz.) packages sliced baby portobello mushrooms
- 3 Tbsp. olive oil
- 6 garlic cloves, peeled and chopped
- 1 (28-oz.) can whole tomatoes, undrained and chopped
- ½ tsp. table salt
- ½ tsp. freshly ground black pepper
- ¼ cup chopped fresh basil
- 2 Tbsp. butter
- Garnish: fresh basil leaves

1. Cook pasta according to package directions; drain.

2. Cook mushrooms in hot oil in skillet over medium-high heat, stirring often, 10 minutes or until browned. Add garlic and cook 1 to 2 minutes until browned.

3. Add tomatoes, salt, and pepper to mushrooms. Cook over medium heat 5 minutes or until thoroughly heated. Add basil and butter, stirring until butter melts. Serve sauce over pasta.

Sage-Brown Butter Squash Agnolotti

MAKES: 6 SERVINGS **HANDS-ON TIME:** 10 MIN.
TOTAL TIME: 10 MIN.

3 (8-oz.) packages refrigerated roasted butternut squash ravioli or other butternut squash-filled pasta
1 lemon
½ cup butter
2 Tbsp. chopped fresh sage leaves
¼ tsp. garlic salt
¼ tsp. freshly ground black pepper
⅓ cup toasted chopped walnuts

Garnish: fresh sage leaves

1. Cook pasta according to package directions; drain.

2. Grate zest from lemon to equal 1 tsp. Cut lemon in half; squeeze juice from lemon into a measuring cup to equal 1½ tsp.

3. Cook butter in a small heavy saucepan over medium heat, stirring constantly, 5 minutes or just until butter begins to turn golden brown. Immediately remove pan from heat. (Butter will continue to darken if left in saucepan.) Stir in lemon zest and juice, sage, garlic salt, and pepper. Drizzle butter mixture over pasta, tossing to coat. Sprinkle with toasted walnuts. Serve immediately.

• Note: We tested with Monterey Gourmet Foods Butternut Squash Ravioli.

Make It A Meal
Serve pasta with a green salad on the side. You can also use other filled pastas, such as mushroom, lobster, or cheese.

Lemon Tortellini with Toasted Crumbs

MAKES: 6 SERVINGS   **HANDS-ON TIME: 14 MIN.**
TOTAL TIME: 14 MIN.

1	(20-oz.) package refrigerated cheese filled tortellini
½	tsp. table salt, divided
½	tsp. freshly ground black pepper, divided
⅔	cup butter, divided
⅔	cup dry Italian-seasoned breadcrumbs
1	lemon
3	garlic cloves, chopped
	Fresh flat-leaf parsley

1. Cook pasta according to package directions; drain. Add ¼ tsp. salt and ¼ tsp. pepper; toss gently. Cover and keep warm.

2. Meanwhile, melt ⅓ cup butter in a medium skillet over medium heat; add breadcrumbs, and cook, stirring constantly, until toasted. Transfer crumb mixture to a small bowl. Wipe skillet clean with a paper towel.

3. Grate zest from lemon to equal 1 Tbsp. Cut lemon in half; squeeze juice from lemon into a measuring cup to equal 1 Tbsp.

4. Melt remaining ⅓ cup butter in skillet over medium heat; add garlic, and sauté 3 minutes. Add lemon zest and juice, remaining ¼ tsp. salt, and remaining ¼ tsp. pepper. Cook, stirring constantly, 2 minutes. Stir in pasta; cook 1 minute. Sprinkle crumb mixture over pasta; sprinkle with parsley. Serve immediately.

From My Kitchen

Toast the crumbs and add them to the dish to provide an element of crunch to an otherwise soft pasta dish, or serve with grilled chicken or steak.

Alfredo Vegetable Pasta

MAKES: 5 servings   **HANDS-ON TIME:** 23 min.
TOTAL TIME: 23 min.

Instead of the usual fettuccine, we used pappardelle pasta for its wide surface area to catch all of the sauce. Serve with crusty, French bread.

1	lb. thin asparagus spears	2	(10-oz.) containers refrigerated Alfredo sauce
1	(8.8-oz.) package pappardelle pasta	½	tsp. freshly ground black pepper
¼	cup butter	⅔	cup freshly grated Parmesan cheese
2	Tbsp. olive oil		
2	(8-oz.) packages sliced baby portobello mushrooms		Garnish: Italian parsley leaves

1. Snap off, and discard tough ends of asparagus. Cut asparagus into 1-inch pieces.

2. Cook pasta in a large pot of boiling salted water according to package directions, adding asparagus during last 2 minutes of cooking. Drain and place in a large bowl.

3. Meanwhile, melt butter with oil in a large skillet over medium-high heat; add mushrooms, and cook, stirring occasionally, 8 minutes or until browned. Reduce heat to medium. Stir in Alfredo sauce and pepper. Bring to a simmer, and cook, stirring occasionally, 3 minutes or until thoroughly heated. Add mushroom sauce to pasta and asparagus; toss gently. Sprinkle with cheese.

Budget Special
Purchase frozen asparagus spears when they are on sale. You can also use canned asparagus spears, drained. Just add them to the pasta water.

Lamb Ragu with Mint

MAKES: 8 SERVINGS **HANDS-ON TIME:** 14 MIN.
TOTAL TIME: 14 MIN.

This serves a crowd, so invite friends who are hearty eaters, and have loaves of crusty hot bread at the ready to sop up the sauce.

16	oz. uncooked rigatoni pasta	2	(24-oz.) jars Cabernet marinara with herbs pasta sauce
1	lb. ground lamb or ground beef		
½	tsp. table salt	½	cup ricotta cheese
¼	tsp. freshly ground black pepper	½	cup fresh mint leaves, torn

1. Cook pasta according to package directions. Drain.

2. Meanwhile, brown ground lamb in a large nonstick skillet over medium-high heat, stirring often, 6 minutes or until lamb crumbles and is no longer pink; drain. Add salt, pepper, and pasta sauce. Bring to a simmer over medium heat; cook stirring occasionally, 4 minutes or until thoroughly heated. Stir in pasta.

3. Dollop tablespoonfuls of ricotta cheese over pasta mixture. Cover and cook 4 minutes. Sprinkle with mint. Serve immediately.

• Note: We tested with Classico Carbernet Marinara with Herbs pasta sauce.

From My Kitchen
Use any tubular-shaped pasta that will hold pockets of this delicious sauce. Replace the lamb with beef and the mint with basil, if you like.

Not Just for Breakfast

Mix up your meals by serving first-of-the-day dishes for dinner.

Spicy Egg and Cheese Croissant

MAKES: 4 SERVINGS   **HANDS-ON TIME: 21 MIN.**
TOTAL TIME: 21 MIN.

6	large eggs	4	(¾-oz.) pepper Jack cheese slices
¼	tsp. table salt	8	cooked bacon slices
¼	tsp. freshly ground pepper	⅓	cup mayonnaise
2	tsp. canola oil	1	tsp. adobo sauce or smoky hot sauce
4	large croissants, warmed and split		

1. Whisk together eggs, salt, and pepper. Heat oil in medium non-stick skillet over medium heat. Add egg mixture to skillet, and cook, without stirring, 30 seconds or until eggs begin to set on bottom. Gently draw cooked edges away from sides of skillet to form large pieces. Cook, stirring occasionally, 1 to 2 minutes or until eggs are thickened and moist. (Do not overstir.)

2. Spoon egg mixture evenly onto cut sides of croissant bottoms; top each with 1 cheese slice and 2 bacon slices.

3. Combine mayonnaise and adobo sauce. Spread evenly over cut sides of croissant tops. Place croissant tops, mayonnaise sides down, on top of bacon.

From My Kitchen

Save leftover chipotle chiles and adobo sauce to stir into mayonnaise or sour cream for a spicy spread or dipping sauce.

Migas

MAKES: 6 SERVINGS **HANDS-ON TIME: 11 MIN.**
TOTAL TIME: 11 MIN.

Serve with chipotle hot sauce, which has a smoky, spicy flavor that goes great with eggs.

1	Tbsp. olive oil	½	cup (2 oz.) shredded sharp
1	(8-oz.) container refriger-		Cheddar cheese
	ated pico de gallo, drained	6	(8-inch) flour tortillas,
6	large eggs		toasted
¼	tsp. table salt	Garnishes: chipotle hot sauce,
½	cup crushed tortilla chips		fresh cilantro leaves

1. Heat oil in a large nonstick skillet over medium-high heat. Add pico de gallo , and cook 3 minutes until liquid evaporates, stirring occasionally. Reduce heat to medium.

2. Whisk together eggs and salt in a bowl until foamy. Add egg mixture to skillet, and cook, without stirring, 2 minutes or until eggs begin to set on bottom. Gently draw cooked edges away from sides of skillet to form large pieces. Add tortilla chips and cheese. Cook, stirring occasionally, until eggs are thickened and moist and cheese melts. Spoon egg mixture evenly into flour tortillas. Fold opposite sides of tortillas over filling, and roll up. Serve immediately.

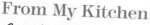

From My Kitchen

Serve these migas with corn tortillas and shredded pepper Jack cheese for a kick.

Eggs in Fire Roasted Tomato Sauce

MAKES: 6 SERVINGS **HANDS-ON TIME:** 21 MIN.
TOTAL TIME: 21 MIN.

Enjoy a very satisfying savory meal with a piece of toasted baguette bread for dipping in the delicious sauce. You can also add a couple tablespoons cooked, crumbled bacon.

2	(14.5-oz) cans diced fire-roasted tomatoes with garlic	½	tsp. freshly ground pepper, divided
2	Tbsp. extra virgin olive oil	12	large eggs
½	tsp. dried oregano	6	Tbsp. freshly grated Parmesan cheese
½	tsp. table salt, divided	6	French bread baguette slices, toasted

1. Preheat oven to 400°. Process first 3 ingredients, ¼ tsp. salt and ¼ tsp. pepper in a blender until smooth. Pour into microwave-safe bowl; cover and microwave at HIGH 2 minutes, stirring after 1 minute.

2. Place 6 (10-oz.) shallow baking dishes on 2 baking sheets. Divide warm sauce among dishes. Break 2 eggs, and slip into sauce in each dish. Sprinkle evenly with remaining ¼ tsp. salt and remaining ¼ tsp. pepper. Sprinkle 1 Tbsp. cheese over eggs in each dish.

3. Bake at 400° for 15 minutes, or until egg whites are set. Serve hot with toasted baguette slices for dipping.

Crustless Spinach Quiche

MAKES: 6 SERVINGS **HANDS-ON TIME:** 10 MIN.
TOTAL TIME: 45 MIN.

Farmer's cheese is actually pressed cottage cheese that can be made from cow, sheep, or goat milk. It is crumbly like feta, with a milder flavor.

2	Tbsp. butter	½	tsp. dried thyme
1	medium onion, chopped	1	tsp. table salt
1	(10-oz.) package frozen chopped spinach, thawed	½	tsp. freshly ground pepper
5	large eggs, lightly beaten	2	cups shredded part-skim farmer's cheese

1. Preheat oven to 350°. Melt butter in a medium skillet. Add onion; sauté 5 minutes or until tender and golden brown. Cool 5 minutes.

2. Drain spinach well, pressing between paper towels. Combine spinach and onion. Spoon into a lightly greased 10-inch pie plate. Whisk together eggs and next 3 ingredients. Stir in cheese; pour over spinach mixture. Bake at 350° for 30 minutes or until center is set. Cool 15 minutes before cutting into wedges.

Budget Special
Add any dried herbs you have on hand to this dish. They will add another element of flavor to this quiche.

Pimiento Cheese Egg Casserole

**MAKES: 6 to 8 servings HANDS-ON TIME: 10 min.
TOTAL TIME: 2 hours, 7 min.**

Stir in cooked, crumbled bacon or sausage for a meaty casserole.

- 1 (5-oz.) package sea salt and pepper-seasoned croutons
- 6 large eggs
- 2½ cups milk
- ¼ tsp. table salt
- ¼ tsp. freshly ground pepper
- 1 (8-oz.) block sharp Cheddar cheese, shredded
- 1 (4-oz.) jar diced pimiento, drained

Garnish: chopped fresh chives

1. Preheat oven to 325°. Place croutons in a lightly greased 11- x 7-inch baking dish.

2. Whisk together eggs and next 3 ingredients in a large bowl. Combine cheese and pimiento in medium bowl. Whisk half of cheese mixture into milk mixture; pour over croutons. Cover and chill 1 hour.

3. Bake, uncovered, at 325° for 45 minutes or until set. Remove from oven; top with remaining cheese mixture. Bake 7 more minutes or until cheese melts. Let stand 5 minutes before serving.

• Note: We tested with New York Texas Toast Sea Salt & Pepper Croutons.

From My Kitchen

Shred your own cheese for this recipe. It will melt better and make the casserole creamier.

Smoked Salmon, Goat Cheese, and Asparagus Frittata

MAKES: 6 SERVINGS   **HANDS-ON TIME:** 10 MIN.
TOTAL TIME: 19 MIN.

This dish would be equally as nice for dinner as for your next brunch for guests.

1	lb. thin fresh asparagus
1	Tbsp. olive oil
3	garlic cloves, minced
10	large eggs
¼	tsp. table salt

¼	tsp. freshly ground pepper
1	(4 oz.) package thinly sliced smoked salmon, chopped
1	(4-oz.) package goat cheese, crumbled

1. Preheat oven to 350° with oven rack 6 inches from top of heat source. Snap off, and discard tough ends of asparagus; cut asparagus into 1-inch pieces.

2. Sauté asparagus in hot oil in a 10-inch ovenproof nonstick skillet over medium-high heat 3 minutes or just until tender. Add garlic; sauté 1 minute.

3. Whisk together eggs, salt, and pepper in a bowl. Stir in salmon. Pour egg mixture over asparagus in skillet; sprinkle with cheese. Cook, stirring occasionally, 2 minutes or until almost set.

4. Bake at 350° for 6 minutes or until set. Increase oven temperature to broil. Broil 3 minutes or until lightly browned.

Budget Special

Substitute feta cheese or chive cream cheese for the goat cheese, if that's what you have on hand.

Spicy Andouille Frittata

MAKES: 6 SERVINGS   **HANDS-ON TIME: 16 MIN.**
TOTAL TIME: 28 MIN.

This quick "frittata for dinner" gets its heat from spicy andouille sausage and a flavor boost from fried peppers and gouda cheese.

½	(16-oz.) package andouille sausage	¼	tsp. table salt
2	tsp. olive oil	¾	cup coarsely chopped drained jarred fried peppers
8	large eggs		
½	cup milk	8	oz. Gouda cheese, shredded and divided
½	tsp. freshly ground pepper		

1. Preheat oven to 350° with oven rack 8 inches from heat. Cut sausage in half lengthwise; cut halves into ¼-inch-thick half-moon slices. Cook sausage in hot oil in a 10-inch ovenproof nonstick skillet over medium-high heat, stirring often, 4 minutes or until browned. Remove sausage with a slotted spoon. Drain on paper towels.

2. Whisk together eggs and next 3 ingredients. Stir in sausage, peppers, and 1¼ cups cheese. Pour egg mixture into skillet. Cook, stirring occasionally, 3 minutes or until almost set.

3. Bake, uncovered, at 350° for 10 minutes or until set. Increase oven temperature to broil; sprinkle top with remaining ¾ cup cheese. Broil 3 minutes or until lightly browned.

• Note: We tested with Savoie's Andouille Sausage and Mancini Fried Peppers.

Make It A Meal
Serve this frittata with a green salad loaded with fresh veggies or a bowl of fresh fruit.

Spinach and Egg Biscuit Cups

MAKES: 6 to 8 servings   HANDS-ON TIME: 11 min.
TOTAL TIME: 36 min.

Reheat any leftover biscuit cups for breakfast the following morning or breakfast on the run.

1 (9-oz.) package frozen creamed spinach	¼ tsp. table salt
6 (⅛-inch-thick) pancetta slices or bacon	¼ tsp. freshly ground pepper
8 large eggs, lightly beaten	2 (7.5-oz.) cans refrigerated buttermilk biscuits
1 cup (4 oz.) shredded fontina cheese	Cooking spray

1. Preheat oven to 350°. Cook spinach according to package directions. Cool 5 minutes.

2. Meanwhile, cook pancetta in a large nonstick skillet over medium heat 6 to 8 minutes or until crisp; drain on paper towels. Crumble pancetta.

3. Combine spinach, pancetta, eggs, and next 3 ingredients in a medium bowl.

4. Roll out biscuits into 3-inch circles. Press circles in bottoms and three-quarters of the way up sides of 20 muffin cups coated with cooking spray. Divide egg mixture evenly among biscuit cups.

5. Bake at 350° for 20 minutes or until biscuits are golden brown and filling is set.

Budget Special
Save some money at the grocery store by swapping out regular cooked crumbled bacon for the pancetta.

Bacon and Eggs Bread Pudding

**MAKES: 4 TO 6 SERVINGS HANDS-ON TIME: 7 MIN.
TOTAL TIME: 47 MIN.**

This quick, easy dish is a great way to use up day-old bread.

4	large eggs
1	cup milk
⅓	cup freshly grated Parmesan cheese
3	Tbsp. butter, melted
1	tsp. salt
½	tsp. freshly ground pepper

⅓	cup sliced green onions (optional)
5	hickory-smoked bacon slices, cooked and crumbled
½	(16-oz.) French bread loaf, cut into 1-inch cubes

1. Preheat oven to 350°. Whisk first 6 ingredients and, if desired, green onions. Add bacon and bread cubes; toss well to coat. Spoon bread mixture into a lightly greased 11- x 7-inch baking dish. Let stand at room temperature, 10 minutes.

2. Bake, uncovered, at 350° for 30 minutes or until golden brown and set in center.

From My Kitchen

Use this recipe as a base to create other delicious savory bread puddings using your family's favorite ingredients.

Carmelized Leek and Fontina Quiche

MAKES: 6 SERVINGS   **HANDS-ON TIME:** 20 MIN.
TOTAL TIME: I HOUR, 26 MIN.

This easy quiche, filled with caramelized leeks and creamy fontina cheese, makes a good meal any time of day.

½   (14.1-oz.) package refrigerated piecrusts
3   large leeks (about 1¾ lb.)
I   Tbsp. olive oil
8   oz. (2 cups) fontina cheese, shredded
1¼   cups half-and-half
4   large eggs
½   tsp. table salt
¼   tsp. freshly ground pepper

1. Preheat oven to 425°. Fit piecrust into a 9-inch pie plate; fold edges under and crimp. Line pastry with aluminum foil, and fill with pie weights or dried beans.

2. Bake at 425° for 8 minutes. Remove weights and foil, and bake 3 more minutes or until bottom is golden brown. Remove from oven. Place on a wire rack, and cool completely (about 15 minutes). Reduce oven temperature to 350°.

3. Meanwhile, remove and discard root ends and dark green tops of leeks. Cut in half lengthwise, and rinse thoroughly under cold running water to remove grit and sand. Thinly slice leeks. Cook leeks in hot oil in a large nonstick skillet over medium-high heat, stirring often, 10 minutes or until leeks are caramel colored. Remove from heat. Place half of leeks in piecrust, and top with half of cheese; repeat with remaining leeks and cheese.

4. Whisk together half-and-half and next 3 ingredients; pour over cheese.

5. Bake at 350° for 40 minutes or until set. Cool on a wire rack 15 minutes before serving.

From My Kitchen
Substitute mild provolone or Gouda for the fontina cheese. To reheat, microwave quiche in 30-second intervals until hot.

Cheesy Southwestern Hash Browns with Sausage

MAKES: 4 servings   **HANDS-ON TIME:** 23 min.
TOTAL TIME: 23 min.

Use hot pork sausage instead of mild for an even spicier dish.

- 1 (1-lb.) package mild ground pork sausage
- 1 (8-oz.) package refrigerated prechopped tricolored bell pepper
- 1 (8-oz.) package refrigerated prechopped onion
- 1 (20-oz.) package refriger-ated Southwest-style hash browns
- 3 Tbsp. vegetable oil, divided
- 1 cup (4 oz.) freshly shredded pepper Jack cheese

1. Cook sausage in a large nonstick skillet over medium heat, stirring often, 5 to 6 minutes until sausage crumbles and is no longer pink. Remove sausage from skillet using a slotted spoon; drain on paper towels, reserving 1 Tbsp. drippings in skillet.

2. Add bell pepper and onion to skillet; sauté 6 to 8 minutes or until tender. Remove from skillet, and place in a large bowl. Add sausage and hash browns; toss to combine.

3. Wipe skillet clean with a paper towel. Heat 2 Tbsp. oil in skillet over medium heat. Add hash brown mixture, spreading in an even layer and pressing lightly with a spatula. Cook 4 minutes or until golden brown on bottom. Drizzle with remaining 1 Tbsp. oil; turn potatoes over, one-third portion at a time. Cook 6 minutes or until golden brown and tender. Sprinkle with cheese. Cover and cook 1 minute or until cheese melts.

From My Kitchen
Use shredded Colby Jack or Monterey Jack cheese for a milder flavor.

Sausage Crêpes

MAKES: 4 servings **HANDS-ON TIME:** 30 MIN.
TOTAL TIME: 50 MIN.

1 cup milk	1 (8-oz.) container chive-and-onion cream cheese
⅔ cup all-purpose flour	
3 large eggs	½ tsp. freshly ground pepper
1 (1-lb.) package ground pork sausage	Melted butter
½ cup finely chopped onion	Garnish: chopped fresh chives

1. Process first 3 ingredients in a blender until smooth. Cover and chill 20 minutes.

2. Meanwhile, cook sausage and onion in a large nonstick skillet over medium-high heat, stirring often, 5 minutes or until sausage crumbles and is no longer pink. Drain and return to skillet.

3. Reduce heat to medium. Add cream cheese and pepper to sausage mixture, stirring until cream cheese melts. Remove from heat, and keep warm.

4. Heat a crêpe pan or 8-inch nonstick skillet over medium heat. Brush pan with melted butter.

5. Stir crêpe batter. Pour 2 Tbsp. batter into skillet; quickly tilt in all directions so that batter covers bottom of skillet with a thin film.

6. Cook about 1 minute. Carefully lift edge of crêpe with a spatula to test for doneness. The crêpe is ready to turn when it can be shaken loose from skillet. Turn crêpe over, and cook about 30 to 40 seconds or until done. Repeat procedure with remaining batter. Stack crêpes between sheets of wax paper until ready to fill.

7. Spoon about 2 Tbsp. sausage mixture down center of each crêpe; roll up.

From My Kitchen
You need to grease the crêpe pan each time you make a crêpe by either brushing the pan with butter or using cooking spray.

Potato Nugget Breakfast Tacos

MAKES: 8 servings　　**HANDS-ON TIME:** 23 min.
TOTAL TIME: 23 min.

These breakfast tacos, featuring crispy potato nuggets (a kids' favorite), are equally good for dinner.

3½ cups frozen mini potato nuggets

¼ cup vegetable oil

24 (6-inch) fajita-size corn tortillas

8-oz. lean ham steak, diced

8 large eggs, lightly beaten

1 (16-oz.) container refrigerated medium salsa

Garnish: fresh cilantro

1. Preheat oven to 300°. Cook potato nuggets in hot oil in a large nonstick skillet over medium-high heat, stirring occasionally, 8 minutes or until crisp.

2. Meanwhile, wrap corn tortillas in aluminum foil. Bake at 300° for 5 minutes or until warm.

3. Add ham to skillet, and cook, stirring occasionally, 3 minutes until lightly browned. Reduce heat to medium.

4. Add eggs to skillet, and cook, without stirring, 1 minute or until eggs begin to set on bottom. Gently draw cooked edges away from sides of skillet to form large pieces. Cook, stirring occasionally, 1 minute or until eggs are thickened and moist. (Do not overstir.)

5. Spoon ¼ cup potato mixture over half of each tortilla. Top each with 1 Tbsp. salsa. Fold in half, and serve immediately.

• Note: We tested with Ore-Ida Mini Tater Tots.

From My Kitchen
This recipe can easily be halved for smaller servings.

Sausage and Kale Grits

MAKES: 8 SERVINGS **HANDS-ON TIME:** 23 MIN.
TOTAL TIME: 28 MIN.

Creamy grits topped with sautéed sausage and fresh kale greens make a complete and filling meal.

2	cups half-and-half	¾	lb. fresh kale, washed, trimmed, and chopped
1¾	tsp. table salt, divided		
1½	cups uncooked quick-cooking grits	1	tsp. garlic powder
		¼	tsp. ground pepper
2	Tbsp. butter	1½	cups (6 oz.) shredded Italian six-cheese blend
1	lb. Italian pork sausage		

1. Bring 3 cups water, half-and-half, and 1¼ tsp. salt to a boil in a large saucepan over medium-high heat. Quickly whisk in grits; bring to a boil, stirring constantly. Reduce heat to medium-low, and simmer, uncovered, stirring often, 5 minutes or until thickened. Stir in butter until melted. Cover and keep warm.

2. Brown sausage in a large skillet over medium-high heat, stirring often, 8 to 9 minutes or until meat crumbles and is no longer pink. Remove sausage from skillet using a slotted spoon; reserve 2 Tbsp. drippings in skillet.

3. Preheat broiler with oven rack 3 inches from heat. Remove and discard coarse stems from kale. Heat reserved drippings in skillet over medium-high heat. Cook half of kale and garlic powder in hot drippings, stirring constantly, until kale begins to wilt. Add remaining half of kale, and cook 2 to 3 minutes or until all kale has wilted. Add ⅓ cup water; reduce heat to medium-low. Cover and cook, stirring occasionally, 12 to 15 minutes or until kale is tender. Transfer kale to a large bowl. Stir in grits, sausage, pepper, and remaining ½ tsp. salt. Spoon mixture into 8 (10-oz.) ramekins. Sprinkle evenly with cheese. Broil 1 minute or until cheese melts.

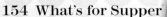

Pigs in a Blanket

MAKES: 4 SERVINGS **HANDS-ON TIME:** 20 MIN.
TOTAL TIME: 20 MIN.

These piggies are a twist on the original favorites you loved as a kid. They make a great option for a satisfying meal in a hurry.

1	(12-oz.) package chicken and apple smoked chicken sausage links, halved crosswise	8	(¾-oz.) slices sharp Cheddar cheese
1	(16.3-oz.) can refrigerated jumbo biscuits	1	(10-oz.) jar jalapeño pepper jelly or red pepper jelly
		¼	cup chopped fresh cilantro

1. Preheat oven to 425°. Cook sausage in a large skillet over medium-high heat, turning often, 3 minutes or until brown.

2. Roll out biscuits into 5-inch circles. Place 1 cheese slice on top of each biscuit; top each with one piece of sausage. Fold biscuit dough over filling; press edges to seal. Place on an ungreased baking sheet.

3. Bake at 425° for 12 minutes or until golden brown.

4. Place jelly in a small microwave-safe bowl. Microwave at HIGH 1 minute or until jelly melts, stirring after 30 seconds. Stir in cilantro. Serve cilantro sauce with pigs in blankets.

• Note: We tested with Grands! Refrigerated Biscuits.

From My Kitchen

Serve these at your next party. Just double or triple the ingredients based on the number in your crowd.

Bacon and Cheddar Belgian Waffles

MAKES: 6 SERVINGS **HANDS-ON TIME: 18 MIN.**
TOTAL TIME: 18 MIN.

1	(2.52-oz.) package precooked bacon	1	cup (4 oz.) shredded sharp Cheddar cheese
2	cups all-purpose baking mix	1	large egg, lightly beaten
		1½	cups milk
		¼	cup butter, melted

1. Prepare bacon according to package directions; chop.

2. Stir together baking mix, cheese, and bacon. Whisk together egg, milk, and melted butter in small bowl; whisk into dry ingredients.

3. Cook batter in a preheated, oiled Belgian-style waffle iron until golden (about 1¼ cups batter each, spreading slightly). Serve with butter and maple syrup, if desired.

• Note: If you don't have a Belgian waffle iron, use ½ cup batter for each waffle in a traditional waffle iron.

Make It A Meal

Round out your meal by serving these waffles with seasonal fresh fruit, and top them with fried eggs.

Oatmeal Waffles with Sautéed Apples

MAKES: 6 SERVINGS   **HANDS-ON TIME:** 21 MIN.
TOTAL TIME: 33 MIN.

1	cup uncooked quick-cooking oats	½	tsp. ground cinnamon
1	cup apple juice	¼	cup butter
2	cups just-add-water pancake mix	2	Gala apples, peeled and sliced
⅓	cup vegetable oil	½	cup firmly packed light brown sugar

1. Preheat oven to 350°. Place oats on jelly-roll pan. Bake for 6 to 7 minutes or until toasted, stirring halfway through. Cool for 5 minutes.

2. Microwave apple juice in a 1-cup glass measuring cup at HIGH 1 to 2 minutes or until warm.

3. Combine pancake mix, oil, cinnamon, toasted oats, warm apple juice, and 1 cup water. Cook batter in a preheated, oiled Belgian-style waffle iron until golden (about ⅓ cup batter per waffle).

4. Melt butter in medium nonstick skillet over medium heat. Add apple slices and brown sugar to skillet. Cook, stirring occasionally, 5 to 6 minutes or until apple is tender and beginning to brown. Serve sautéed apples over waffles.

• Note: We tested with Krusteaz Buttermilk Pancake Mix.

From My Kitchen
Buy bags of peeled, sliced apples in the produce department to speed up prep.

Apricot-Almond French Toast

MAKES: 4 SERVINGS　　**HANDS-ON TIME:** 27 MIN.
TOTAL TIME: 27 MIN.

Apricot and almond, a classic flavor combination, marry deliciously in this quick, simple French toast.

1　cup melted vanilla ice
　　cream
2　large eggs
½　cup sliced almonds

2　Tbsp. sugar
8　(1-inch-thick) challah
　　bread slices
½　cup apricot preserves

1. Whisk together ice cream and eggs in a bowl. Combine almonds and sugar in a shallow dish. Dip bread slices into egg mixture, coating well. Lightly press 1 side of bread slices, 1 at a time, into almond mixture.

2. Cook bread, in batches, in a lightly greased nonstick skillet or griddle over medium-low heat 1 to 2 minutes on each side or until golden brown.

3. Microwave apricot preserves and 2 Tbsp. water in a 1-cup glass measuring cup at HIGH 30 seconds to 1 minute or until smooth, stirring at 30-second intervals. Top French toast with apricot syrup.

Budget Special
Substitute day-old or leftover bread in place of the challah.

Monte Cristo French Toast

MAKES: 6 SERVINGS **HANDS-ON TIME: 13 MIN.**
TOTAL TIME: 13 MIN.

6	(1½-inch-thick) diagonally-cut French bread slices	4	large eggs
½	lb. shaved deli ham	1½	cups half-and-half
1	cup (4 oz.) Gruyère cheese, grated		Powdered sugar
			Jam or preserves

1. Cut a slit into top crust of each bread slice to form a pocket. Stuff ham and cheese evenly into pockets.

2. Whisk together eggs and half-and-half in shallow dish. Lightly press bread slices, 1 at a time, into egg mixture, coating both sides of bread.

3. Cook bread, in batches, on a lightly greased nonstick griddle over medium heat 3 to 4 minutes on each side or until done and cheese melts. Dust with powdered sugar, and serve with jam or preserves.

• Note: We tested with Boar's Head Tavern Ham.

From My Kitchen

Choose a savory ham as opposed to a honey or maple deli ham. Serve with your favorite jam or preserves.

Peach Pancakes

MAKES: 6 SERVINGS   **HANDS-ON TIME:** 20 MIN.
TOTAL TIME: 22 MIN.

2	cups chopped fresh or frozen peaches, divided	¼	tsp. ground ginger
¼	cup firmly packed light brown sugar, divided	2	cups just-add-water pancake mix
		2	cups peach nectar, divided

1. Stir together I cup peaches, 2 Tbsp. brown sugar, and ginger. Stir together pancake mix, I cup peach nectar, and ½ cup water. Stir in peach mixture.

2. Combine remaining I cup peaches, remaining 2 Tbsp. brown sugar, and remaining I cup peach nectar in a small saucepan. Bring to a boil over medium heat; cook, stirring occasionally, 5 minutes or until syrupy.

3. Pour about ¼ cup batter for each pancake onto a hot, lightly greased griddle or large nonstick skillet. Cook pancakes over medium heat 2 minutes or until tops are covered with bubbles and edges look dry and cooked; turn and cook other side about 30 seconds. Serve with remaining peach syrup.

• Note: We tested with Krusteaz Buttermilk Pancake Mix.

From My Kitchen

Use frozen peaches if fresh peaches are unavailable. Substitute cinnamon for the ginger.

Dinner in a Dish

Prepare one simple recipe
to enjoy one delicious meal.

Baked Beef and Fried Pepper Burritos

MAKES: 4 SERVINGS   **HANDS-ON TIME: 9 MIN.**
TOTAL TIME: 19 MIN.

I   (15-oz.) package fully cooked beef roast au jus, drained

I   cup (4 oz.) shredded Mexican four-cheese blend

½   cup drained jarred fried peppers

½   cup corn and black bean salsa

4   (9-inch) soft taco-size flour tortillas

Cooking spray

1. Preheat oven to 400°. Shred beef with 2 forks.

2. Place ⅓ cup beef, ¼ cup cheese, 2 Tbsp. peppers, and 2 Tbsp. salsa just below center of each tortilla. Fold opposite sides of tortilla over filling, and roll up. Place burritos on a lightly greased baking sheet. Coat tops of burritos with cooking spray. Bake at 400° for 10 minutes or until tops are golden brown.

• Note: We tested with Mancini Fried Peppers.

From My Kitchen

Top each burrito with sour cream and your favorite salsa for a lighter version of this popular dish.

Beef Stroganoff

MAKES: 6 SERVINGS   **HANDS-ON TIME:** 24 MIN.
TOTAL TIME: 34 MIN.

Serve over hot cooked egg noodles.

¼	cup all-purpose flour	1	cup beef broth
1	tsp. table salt	2	Tbsp. tomato paste
1	tsp. freshly ground black pepper	1	(10½-oz.) can condensed beefy mushroom soup
2	lb. top sirloin steak, cut into thin slices	1	(8-oz.) container sour cream
3	Tbsp. olive oil		

1. Combine first 3 ingredients in a shallow dish. Dredge beef in flour mixture, shaking off excess. Heat 1½ Tbsp. oil in a large nonstick skillet over high heat. Add half of steak; cook, stirring often, 6 minutes or until steak is browned. Remove steak from skillet. Repeat procedure with remaining 1½ Tbsp. oil and remaining half of steak.

2. Add broth, tomato paste, and soup. Cook 1 minute, whisking to loosen browned bits from bottom of skillet. Return beef to skillet; cover and cook, stirring occasionally, 10 minutes or until meat is tender and sauce is slightly thickened, stirring occasionally. Remove from heat, and let stand 5 minutes. Stir in sour cream.

From My Kitchen
Buy a tube of tomato paste to keep in the refrigerator for when a recipe calls for just 1 or 2 tablespoons.

Sloppy Joe Biscuit Pie

MAKES: 6 SERVINGS **HANDS-ON TIME: 12 MIN.**
TOTAL TIME: 32 MIN.

Kids and grown-ups alike will dig into this classic favorite dish.
Instead of serving the sloppy Joe mixture on a bun, it's baked
in a pan and topped with biscuits.

1¼	lb. ground round	1	cup (4 oz.) shredded sharp
1	large onion, chopped		Cheddar cheese
1	(15-oz.) can sloppy Joe	1	(16.3-oz.) can refrigerated
	sauce		jumbo buttermilk biscuits

1. Preheat oven to 400°. Brown ground beef and onion in a 12-inch
cast-iron or other ovenproof skillet over medium-high heat, stirring
often, 5 minutes or until meat crumbles and is no longer pink; drain.

2. Return beef mixture to skillet. Stir in sloppy Joe sauce and cheese.
Place biscuits on top of beef mixture.

3. Bake, uncovered, at 400° for 15 minutes or until biscuits are
golden brown. Let stand 5 minutes before serving.

• Note: We tested with Hunt's Manwich Original Sloppy Joe Sauce
and Pillsbury Grands! Buttermilk Biscuits.

From My Kitchen
Buy prechopped onion and
preshredded cheese to save
time on this one-dish favorite.

Fried Apple Pork Chops

MAKES: 4 SERVINGS   **HANDS-ON TIME: 13 MIN.**
TOTAL TIME: 13 MIN.

4 bone-in center-cut pork loin chops (about 2¾ lb.)	2 Tbsp. canola oil
½ tsp. table salt	½ cup apple cider
½ tsp. freshly ground black pepper	1 (15-oz.) can fried apples
	2 Tbsp. butter
	Garnish: fresh thyme leaves

1. Sprinkle pork chops on both sides with salt and pepper. Heat oil in a large nonstick skillet over medium-high heat. Add pork chops; cook 4 minutes on each side or until golden brown. Remove pork chops from pan; keep warm.

2. Add apple cider to pan; reduce heat to low. Cook 30 seconds, stirring to loosen browned bits from bottom of skillet. Return pork chops to skillet; add fried apples. Cook 2 minutes or until apples are thoroughly heated, breaking up apples with a spoon during cooking. Stir in butter until melted. Serve pork chops with sauce.

Make It A Meal

Serve this dish over hot cooked rice to soak up the sauce. Round out the meal with a spinach salad.

Pulled-Pork Shepherd's Pie

MAKES: 4 TO 6 SERVINGS　　　**HANDS-ON TIME: 5 MIN.**
TOTAL TIME: 35 MIN.

1 lb. hickory-cooked pulled pork barbecue	1 cup barbecue sauce
1 (11-oz.) can yellow corn with red and green bell peppers, drained	1 (24-oz.) container refrigerated mashed potatoes
	1 cup (4 oz.) shredded Cheddar cheese

1. Preheat oven to 350°. Stir together first 3 ingredients in a lightly greased 8-inch baking dish. Stir potatoes well; spread over pork mixture.

2. Bake, uncovered, at 350° for 20 minutes. Remove from oven; sprinkle with cheese. Bake 10 more minutes or until cheese melts and casserole is bubbly.

• Note: We tested with Bishop's Hickory Cooked, Vacuum Packed Pork Barbecue and Stubb's Bar-B-Q Sauce.

Budget Special
Use leftover, homemade potatoes instead of buying packaged mashed potatoes. Add fresh herbs to potatoes for extra flavor.

Ham and Cheese Biscuit Casserole

MAKES: 8 SERVINGS   **HANDS-ON TIME:** 10 MIN.
TOTAL TIME: 49 MIN.

1	cup frozen baby English peas, thawed	2	(8-oz.) packages diced cooked ham
¼	tsp. freshly ground black pepper	8	oz. smoked Gouda cheese, shredded and divided
2	(18.5-oz.) cans creamy loaded potato soup	1	(16.3-oz.) can refrigerated jumbo buttermilk biscuits

1. Preheat oven to 375°. Stir together first 4 ingredients and 1½ cups cheese in large bowl. Pour mixture into a lightly greased 13- x 9-inch baking dish. Bake, uncovered, at 375° for 15 minutes.

2. Arrange biscuits over hot soup mixture. Bake, uncovered, 22 more minutes or until biscuits are golden. Sprinkle with remaining ½ cup cheese. Bake 2 more minutes or until cheese melts.

• Note: We tested with Progresso Creamy Loaded Potato Soup and Pillsbury Grand! Refrigerated Biscuits.

From My Kitchen

Serve this creamy casserole with all your favorite baked potato toppings. Try sliced green onions, bacon bits, or grated cheese.

Creamy Chicken-Mushroom Pot Pie

MAKES: 6 SERVINGS **HANDS-ON TIME: 12 MIN.**
TOTAL TIME: 40 MIN.

1	Tbsp. butter
1	(8-oz.) package sliced baby portobello mushrooms
3	cups shredded deli-roasted chicken breast
1½	cups frozen peas and carrots, thawed
¼	tsp. ground black pepper
1	(18-oz.) can creamy portobello mushroom cooking sauce
½	(17.3-oz.) package frozen puff pastry sheets, thawed

1. Preheat oven to 375°. Melt butter in a large skillet over medium heat. Sauté mushroom in melted butter 6 minutes or until tender.

2. Stir together mushrooms, chicken, and next 3 ingredients in a bowl. Spoon mushroom mixture into 6 lightly greased (6-oz.) ramekins.

3. Roll out pastry to a 14- x 10-inch rectangle. Cut pastry into 6 squares. Place 1 square over each ramekin, pressing edges gently to seal pastry to ramekin. Cut slits in tops for steam to escape.

4. Place ramekins on a baking sheet. Bake at 375° for 28 minutes or until golden.

• Note: We tested with Progresso Creamy Portobella Recipe Starters Cooking Sauce.

From My Kitchen

Make 1 large pie. Spoon mixture into a lightly greased 11- x 7-inch baking dish. Roll pastry to a rectangle, and place over dish. Cut slits in top, and bake as directed for 32 minutes.

Chicken Enchilada Suizas

**MAKES: 4 to 6 servings   HANDS-ON TIME: 10 min.
TOTAL TIME: 45 min.**

6   cups chopped cooked chicken

3   cups salsa verde, divided

2   (8-oz.) blocks pepper Jack cheese, shredded and divided

8   (8-inch) flour tortillas

1   (15-oz.) container crema Mexicana or sour cream

Garnish: chopped fresh cilantro

1. Preheat oven to 375°. Combine chicken, 2 cups salsa, and half of cheese. Spoon chicken mixture evenly down center of tortillas, and roll up. Place tortillas, seam side down, in a lightly greased 13- x 9-inch baking dish.

2. Bake, uncovered, at 375° for 20 minutes or until tortillas are beginning to crisp. Combine crema Mexicana and remaining 1 cup salsa; pour over tortillas. Sprinkle with remaining half of cheese. Bake 15 more minutes or until bubbly and cheese melts.

Chicken Thighs and Potatoes

MAKES: 3 SERVINGS   **HANDS-ON TIME:** 18 MIN.
TOTAL TIME: 1 HOUR

6	skinned and boned chicken thighs (1¾ lb.)	1	lb. baby Yukon gold potatoes, halved
1	tsp. garlic salt	1	Tbsp. fresh thyme leaves, divided
½	tsp. freshly ground black pepper	⅓	cup honey mustard
1	Tbsp. olive oil	3	Tbsp. heavy cream

1. Preheat oven to 450°. Sprinkle chicken with garlic salt and pepper. Heat oil in a 12-inch cast-iron or ovenproof skillet over medium-high heat. Add chicken, and cook 4 minutes on each side or until browned. Add potatoes, and sprinkle with 2 tsp. thyme.

2. Bake, uncovered, at 450° for 20 minutes. Remove skillet from oven; stir potatoes. Return skillet to oven, and cook 15 more minutes or until chicken and potatoes are desired degree of doneness.

3. Meanwhile, whisk together mustard, cream, and remaining 1 tsp. thyme in a microwave-safe bowl. Microwave at HIGH 30 to 45 seconds or until warm. Serve with chicken and potatoes.

From My Kitchen
Select a honey mustard that has a creamy consistency for best results with this recipe.

Chicken Kabobs

MAKES: 4 SERVINGS **HANDS-ON TIME: 14 MIN.**
TOTAL TIME: 14 MIN.

You can find mini peppers, which come in a bag, in most grocery stores. Since you only need 8, cut up leftover mini peppers in salads, or stuff them with pimiento cheese, and cook them on the grill.

Cooking spray

2 skinned and boned chicken breasts, cut into 1½-inch pieces

8 red, yellow, and orange sweet mini peppers

1 red onion, cut into 8 wedges

½ large zucchini, cut into ¼-inch slices

4 (8-inch) metal skewers

½ cup red pepper jelly

1. Coat a cold cooking grate with cooking spray, and place on grill. Preheat grill to 350° to 400° (medium-high) heat. Thread chicken and vegetables alternately onto skewers.

2. Place skewers on grill. Grill, covered with grill lid, 8 to 10 minutes or until chicken reaches desired degree of doneness, turning twice. Remove from grill.

3. Melt jelly in a small saucepan over low heat, stirring occasionally. Brush jelly over kabobs.

From My Kitchen

Skewer the zucchini so they lay flat on the grill. Otherwise, the ends will be between the grates and get burned.

Chicken Tortilla Soup

MAKES: 8 servings **HANDS-ON TIME: 9 min.**
TOTAL TIME: 19 min.

3   cups shredded deli-roasted chicken

2   (4.5-oz.) cans chopped green chiles

1   (32-oz.) package chicken broth

1   (12-oz.) package frozen seasoned corn and black beans, thawed

3   cups tortilla chips, coarsely crushed

Garnish: chopped avocado, tomatoes

1. Combine first 4 ingredients in a Dutch oven. Cook over medium heat 10 minutes or until thoroughly heated.

2. Ladle soup into serving bowls. Top with chips.

From My Kitchen

Stir in hominy for extra flavor. Top the soup with cubed avocado and chopped fresh cilantro for added color and flavor.

Turkey Mole Soup

MAKES: 7 CUPS   **HANDS-ON TIME:** 4 MIN.
TOTAL TIME: 19 MIN.

Mole (MOLE-lay) is a rich pepper sauce used in Mexican cooking. It has a secret ingredient…chocolate.

1 Tbsp. olive oil	½ tsp. freshly ground black pepper
1 lb. ground turkey	
1 (8-oz.) container refrigerated prechopped celery, onion, and green bell pepper mix	2 (14½-oz.) cans chicken broth
	1 (15-oz.) can black beans, drained
2 garlic cloves, minced	Garnish: chopped fresh cilantro, chips, and sour cream.
½ cup bottled mole sauce	
½ tsp. table salt	

1. Heat oil in Dutch oven over medium-high heat. Add turkey and celery mix; cook, stirring occasionally, until turkey crumbles and is no longer pink. Add garlic; cook, stirring constantly, 1 minute. Add mole sauce and remaining ingredients. Bring to a simmer; cook, uncovered, stirring occasionally, 15 minutes or until thoroughly heated.

Make It A Meal

Serve this Mexican-inspired soup with tortilla chips and top with sour cream and chopped cilantro.

From My Kitchen

If you substitute low-fat coconut milk, the dish will be spicier.

Creamy Thai Curry Shrimp Soup

MAKES: 6 SERVINGS **HANDS-ON TIME: 15 MIN.**
TOTAL TIME: 15 MIN.

1 cup fresh snow peas	2 (13.5-oz.) cans coconut milk
1 small red bell pepper, chopped	2 Tbsp. soy sauce
2 Tbsp. canola oil	1 lb. peeled medium-size raw shrimp
2 (9-oz.) packages Thai green curry skillet sauce	Garnish: fresh cilantro leaves

1. Trim ends and remove strings from snow peas; discard ends and strings. Cut snow peas lengthwise into thin slices. Sauté snow pea slices and bell pepper in hot oil in a Dutch oven over medium heat 5 minutes or until crisp-tender.

2. Stir together skillet sauce, coconut milk, and soy sauce. Add snow pea mixture; bring to a simmer. Add shrimp; cook 2 minutes or just until shrimp turn pink.

• Note: We tested with Campbell's Thai Green Curry Skillet Sauce.

Baked Shrimp Risotto

MAKES: 4 SERVINGS **HANDS-ON TIME:** 12 MIN.
TOTAL TIME: 52 MIN.

No more standing at the stove and stirring risotto constantly. This super-easy oven risotto is a one-pot dish, ready to bake in just 12 minutes.

⅓	cup butter	2	tsp. fresh thyme leaves
4	garlic cloves, pressed	¼	tsp. table salt
1	cup Arborio rice	¼	tsp. freshly ground
4	cups chicken broth		black pepper
1	lb. peeled and deveined	½	cup grated Parmesan
	large raw shrimp		cheese

1. Preheat oven to 375°. Melt butter in a large ovenproof Dutch oven over medium-high heat. Add garlic, and sauté 1 minute. Add rice, and cook, stirring often, 2 minutes or until rice is toasted. Stir in chicken broth. Bring to a boil; cover and bake at 375° for 25 minutes or until liquid is almost absorbed.

2. Remove from oven. Stir in shrimp; cover and bake 5 more minutes. Remove from oven, and let stand, covered, 10 minutes.

3. Uncover; stir in thyme, salt, and pepper. Sprinkle with cheese.

Budget Special
Omit the shrimp and stir in cooked vegetables or chopped deli-roasted chicken instead.

Herbed Mussels

MAKES: 4 SERVINGS **HANDS-ON TIME:** 13 MIN.
TOTAL TIME: 28 MIN.

⅓ cup butter, divided
4 garlic cloves, sliced
4 fresh thyme sprigs
1½ cups chicken broth
½ cup dry white wine

2 lb. fresh mussels, scrubbed and debearded
Garnish: chopped fresh parsley

1. Melt 2 Tbsp. butter in a Dutch oven over medium-high heat. Add garlic and sauté 2 minutes or until golden brown. Add thyme sprigs, chicken broth, and wine; bring to a boil. Add mussels; cover and cook 5 to 6 minutes or until all mussels have opened. Transfer mussels to 4 shallow serving bowls, reserving broth in Dutch oven.

2. Boil broth, uncovered, until reduced to 1 cup. Whisk in remaining butter. Remove from heat. Spoon broth evenly over mussels. Serve immediately.

Budget Special
Use a mix of whatever herbs you have on hand in place of the thyme.

Roasted Tilapia with Mandarin Salsa

MAKES: 4 SERVINGS **HANDS-ON TIME:** 7 MIN.
TOTAL TIME: 15 MIN.

Mandarin oranges are sweet and full of vitamin C, making this salsa-topped fish not only delicious, but also super healthy.

2 (15-oz.) cans mandarin oranges in light syrup, undrained	¾ tsp. table salt, divided
	4 (6-oz.) tilapia fillets
¼ cup chopped fresh parsley, divided	½ tsp. freshly ground black pepper, divided
2 Tbsp. chopped shallot	2 cups hot cooked jasmine rice
2 Tbsp. extra virgin olive oil, divided	

1. Drain oranges, reserving 2 Tbsp. syrup. Whisk together reserved syrup, 2 Tbsp. chopped parsley, shallot, 1 Tbsp. olive oil, and ¼ tsp. salt in a medium bowl. Add oranges; toss gently.

2. Heat a large nonstick skillet over medium-high heat. Add remaining 1 Tbsp. olive oil to skillet, tilting in all directions to coat bottom of skillet.

3. Sprinkle fillets evenly with ¼ tsp. salt and ¼ tsp. pepper. Cook fish in hot oil 4 minutes on each side or just until fish flakes with a fork.

4. Toss together rice, remaining 2 Tbsp. parsley, remaining ¼ tsp. salt, and remaining ¼ tsp. pepper. Spoon rice evenly onto 4 plates. Top each serving with 1 fillet and ½ cup mandarin salsa.

From My Kitchen
Use 2 (8.8-oz.) packages of precooked jasmine rice for an even quicker meal prep.

Poached Halibut and Veggies

MAKES: 4 SERVINGS   **HANDS-ON TIME:** 5 MIN.
TOTAL TIME: 16 MIN.

¼ cup butter	¼ tsp. table salt
2 (8-oz.) packages steam-in-bag fresh French green beans	¼ tsp. freshly ground black pepper
4 (6-oz.) halibut fillets	1 cup chicken broth
1½ tsp. lemon-herb seasoning	1 cup white wine
	Garnish: lemon wedges

1. Melt butter in a large nonstick skillet over medium heat. Add green beans; sauté 5 minutes.

2. Sprinkle fish with lemon-herb seasoning, salt, and pepper. Add chicken broth and white wine to green beans. Bring to a boil; add fish, skin side down. Cover, reduce heat, and simmer 6 minutes or until fish flakes with a fork.

• Note: We tested with McCormick Lemon Herb Seasoning.

From My Kitchen
Ask the staff at your grocery's seafood counter to remove the skin from halibut. It will make this dish look much nicer.

Chorizo and Potato Soup

MAKES: 6 SERVINGS **HANDS-ON TIME: 5 MIN.**
TOTAL TIME: 20 MIN.

1   (16-oz.) package chorizo
     sausage, casings removed
4   cups chicken broth
1   (20-oz.) package refriger-
     ated Southwest-style hash
     browns

1   (16-oz.) can pinto beans,
     drained and rinsed
½   cup chopped fresh cilantro
Garnishes: sour cream,
     chopped avocado,
     shredded cheese

1. Cook sausage in a Dutch oven over medium heat, stirring often,
8 minutes or until meat crumbles and is no longer pink; drain well.
Return sausage to Dutch oven. Stir in broth, potatoes, and beans.
Bring to a boil; reduce heat, and simmer 10 minutes or until
potatoes are tender.

2. Ladle soup into bowls, and sprinkle evenly with chopped
cilantro.

• Note: We tested with Simply Potatoes Southwest Style Hash
Browns and Cuervito Morado Chorizo sausage.

From My Kitchen

*Make a toppings bar to go
along with this soup. Be sure
to include sour cream, chopped
avocado, and shredded cheese.*

One Pot Mac and Cheese

MAKES: 6 SERVINGS   **HANDS-ON TIME:** 10 MIN.
TOTAL TIME: 28 MIN.

1	lb. uncooked orecchiette pasta	½	tsp. freshly ground black pepper
⅓	cup butter	8	oz. extra-sharp Cheddar cheese, shredded
1½	cups milk		
¾	tsp. table salt	8	oz. Gruyère cheese, shredded

1. Cook pasta according to package directions. Drain pasta, and return to pan. Add butter; cook over medium-low heat, stirring, 1 minute or until butter melts. Add milk and remaining ingredients. Cook, stirring constantly, 4 minutes or until cheese melts and mixture is creamy. Let stand 5 minutes before serving.

Make It A Meal
Round out this stove-top mac and cheese by stirring in cooked broccoli, peas, or spinach with the cooked pasta.

Tortellini Tomato Soup

MAKES: 6 SERVINGS
TOTAL TIME: 9 MIN.

HANDS-ON TIME: 2 MIN.

1½	cups canned crushed tomatoes with basil
1	cup whipping cream
¼	tsp. table salt
¼	tsp. freshly ground black pepper

2	(11-oz.) cans condensed tomato bisque soup, undiluted
¼	cup jarred pesto sauce
1	(9-oz.) package refrigerated cheese-filled tortellini

Garnish: fresh basil leaves

1. Combine first 6 ingredients and 1 cup water in a 4-qt. saucepan; cover and bring to a boil over high heat. Add pasta; reduce heat to medium, and cook, partially covered, 7 minutes or until pasta is tender.

From My Kitchen

Add cooked, crumbled Italian sausage to this soup for extra protein.

Ravioli with Heirloom Tomatoes

MAKES: 4 SERVINGS **HANDS-ON TIME:** 10 MIN.
TOTAL TIME: 55 MIN.

1	lb. heirloom tomatoes, halved	2	Tbsp. balsamic vinegar
2	shallots, sliced	¼	tsp. kosher salt
	Cooking spray	¼	tsp. black pepper
3	Tbsp. extra virgin olive oil, divided	12	oz. 4-cheese ravioli
			Garnishes: basil leaves and shaved Parmesan cheese

1. Preheat oven to 425°.

2. Arrange tomatoes and shallots on a jelly-roll pan coated with cooking spray. Drizzle with 1 Tbsp. oil; toss. Bake at 425° for 35 minutes.

3. Add remaining 2 Tbsp. oil, vinegar, salt, and pepper to pan. Bake 10 more minutes.

4. Cook ravioli according to package directions, omitting salt and fat. Drain ravioli. Transfer ravioli to a serving platter; top with tomato mixture.

King Ranch Skillet Casserole

MAKES: 4 SERVINGS   **HANDS-ON TIME:** 16 MIN.
TOTAL TIME: 16 MIN.

With the help of a flavorful prepared sauce, this classic family-favorite casserole is now just 5 ingredients.

- 1 (8-oz.) package refrigerated prechopped celery, onion, and green bell pepper mix
- 2 Tbsp. canola oil
- 3 cups shredded deli-roasted chicken
- 1 (9-oz.) package creamy chipotle skillet sauce
- 6 (6-inch) corn tortillas, torn into 1-inch pieces
- 1½ cups (6 oz.) shredded Mexican cheese blend

1. Sauté celery mix in hot oil in a large nonstick skillet over medium-high heat 4 minutes or until tender. Add chicken, skillet sauce, and tortilla pieces, stirring well. Cover, reduce heat, and simmer 5 minutes. Uncover, sprinkle with cheese, and simmer 3 more minutes or until cheese melts.

• Note: We tested with Campbell's Creamy Chipotle Skillet Sauce.

From My Kitchen
Top the casserole with about 2 cups of crushed tortilla chips for a bit of added crunch.

So Easy Sides

Round out your meal
with a vegetable or salad.

Lemon and Shallot Brussels Sprouts

MAKES: 4 SERVINGS **HANDS-ON TIME:** 19 MIN.
TOTAL TIME: 19 MIN.

1	lb. fresh Brussels sprouts	¼	tsp. freshly ground pepper
2	Tbsp. olive oil	1	Tbsp. lemon zest
2	Tbsp. chopped shallots	2	Tbsp. fresh lemon juice
½	tsp. table salt	2	Tbsp. butter

1. Remove discolored leaves from Brussels sprouts. Cut off stem ends, and cut lengthwise into quarters.

2. Heat oil in a large skillet over medium-high heat. Add shallots; sauté 3 minutes or until crisp-tender. Reduce heat to medium; add Brussels sprouts, salt, and pepper. Cook, stirring often, 8 minutes or until brown. Add lemon zest and juice; cook 1 minute. Add butter, tossing until melted. Serve immediately.

From My Kitchen
Substitute finely chopped onion for the shallots, if you would like.

Oven-Roasted Asparagus with Dijon Vinaigrette

MAKES: 4 SERVINGS **HANDS-ON TIME:** 4 MIN.
TOTAL TIME: 14 MIN.

1 lb. fresh asparagus	1 Tbsp. red wine vinegar
¼ cup olive oil, divided	2 tsp. chopped fresh chives
½ tsp. kosher salt, divided	2 tsp. Dijon mustard
½ tsp. freshly ground pepper, divided	1 garlic clove, minced

1. Preheat oven to 450°. Snap off and discard tough ends of asparagus. Place asparagus on an ungreased baking sheet. Drizzle with 1 Tbsp. oil; sprinkle with ¼ tsp. salt and ¼ tsp. pepper, tossing to coat.

2. Bake at 450° for 10 minutes or just until tender.

3. Whisk together vinegar, next 3 ingredients, remaining 3 Tbsp. oil, remaining ¼ tsp. salt, and remaining ¼ tsp. pepper in a small bowl. Drizzle over asparagus.

From My Kitchen

Trim asparagus by simply holding both ends of each spear with both hands and snapping the spear where it naturally breaks to remove the tough woody part.

Best BBQ Collard Greens

MAKES: 6 SERVINGS   **HANDS-ON TIME: 14 MIN.**
TOTAL TIME: 24 MIN.

Down-home cooked greens are done in under 25 minutes.

2 Tbsp. olive oil	2 cups hickory-cooked
1 small onion, chopped	pulled pork barbecue
1 large garlic clove, minced	3 Tbsp. pepper sauce
1 (1-lb.) bag refrigerated	1 tsp. table salt
chopped collard greens,	½ tsp. freshly ground pepper
coarse stems removed	

1. Heat oil in large skillet over medium-high heat. Add onion and garlic; sauté 2 minutes. Add one-third of greens; sauté 1 minute or until wilted. Repeat procedure with remaining greens, one-third at a time.

2. Add pork, tossing well. Add ¼ cup water; cover and simmer 10 minutes. Uncover; add pepper sauce, and cook until liquid evaporates, about 5 minutes, stirring occasionally. Stir in salt and pepper.

• Note: We tested with Bishop's Hickory Cooked, Vacuum Packed Pork Barbecue.

From My Kitchen

Find bottled pepper sauce (small green hot peppers in vinegar) in the pickle aisle of your local grocery store.

Broccoli Gratin

MAKES: 8 servings **HANDS-ON TIME:** 8 min.
TOTAL TIME: 21 min.

Panko, Japanese-style breadcrumbs, are coarse, airy, and extra-crunchy.

2 (12-oz.) packages steam-in-bag fresh broccoli florets
1 (1.6-oz.) package Alfredo sauce mix
2 cups milk
5 Tbsp. butter, melted and divided

1¼ cups (5 oz.) shredded Cheddar cheese
½ cup panko (Japanese breadcrumbs)

1. Preheat oven to 425°F. Place broccoli packages in microwave according to package directions. Microwave at HIGH 1 minute. Open packages, and transfer broccoli to a bowl.

2. Prepare Alfredo sauce according to package directions. Add milk and 1 Tbsp. butter. Remove from heat, and stir in cheese.

3. Pour cheese sauce over broccoli; toss to coat. Spoon broccoli mixture into a lightly greased 13- x 9-inch baking dish.

4. Combine panko and remaining ¼ cup butter; sprinkle over broccoli mixture. Bake, uncovered, at 425° for 15 minutes or until bubbly.

Creamed Corn

MAKES: 8 SERVINGS **HANDS-ON TIME:** 5 MIN.
TOTAL TIME: 21 MIN.

1 (2-lb.) package frozen Silver Queen corn, thawed	½ tsp. table salt
½ cup chopped onion	½ tsp. freshly ground pepper
½ cup milk	6 cooked bacon slices, crumbled
¼ cup butter	
1 oz. pepper Jack cheese, shredded	

1. Place first 4 ingredients in a Dutch oven. Cook, stirring constantly, over medium heat 12 minutes or until thickened. Remove from heat, and stir in cheese, salt, and pepper. Sprinkle with bacon.

• Note: We tested with Today's Harvest Silver Queen Style Corn.

Make It A Meal

Pair this side with fried chicken and green beans for a delicious Southern-inspired supper.

Grilled Curry Corn

MAKES: 6 SERVINGS **HANDS-ON TIME: 27 MIN.**
TOTAL TIME: 27 MIN.

¼ cup butter, softened	½ tsp. table salt
2 Tbsp. mango chutney	2 Tbsp. chopped fresh
2 tsp. Madras curry powder	cilantro
6 ears white fresh corn	2 limes, cut into wedges

1. Preheat grill to 350° to 400° (medium-high) heat. Stir together first 3 ingredients.

2. Grill corn, covered with grill lid, 20 minutes or until golden brown, turning occasionally. Remove corn from grill. Brush with butter mixture, and sprinkle with salt and cilantro. Serve with lime wedges.

From My Kitchen
Buy fresh, tender ears of corn that have juicy kernels all the way to the tip of the ear for the best flavor.

Simple Herb-Roasted Root Vegetables

MAKES: 4 SERVINGS   **HANDS-ON TIME: 8** MIN.
TOTAL TIME: 38 MIN.

3   medium carrots,
    cut into I-inch pieces

3   medium parsnips,
    cut into I-inch pieces

2   small onions, each
    cut into 8 wedges

I   medium-size sweet potato,
    peeled and cut into I-inch
    cubes

2   Tbsp. olive oil

2   tsp. dried herbes de
    Provence

I   tsp. kosher salt

½   tsp. freshly ground pepper

1. Preheat oven to 425°. Place first 4 ingredients on a large rimmed baking sheet. Drizzle vegetables with oil; sprinkle with herbes de Provence, salt, and pepper. Toss to coat.

2. Bake at 425° for 30 minutes or until tender, stirring after I5 minutes.

From My Kitchen

If you don't have herbes de Provence on hand, use 2 tsp. of a blend of your favorite dried herbs, such as rosemary, basil, thyme, oregano, or fennel seeds.

Balsamic Green Beans with Tomatoes and Feta

MAKES: 4 SERVINGS   **HANDS-ON TIME:** 9 MIN.
TOTAL TIME: 13 MIN.

1 (12-oz.) package steam-in-bag fresh green beans	¼ tsp. table salt
	¼ tsp. freshly ground pepper
1 Tbsp. olive oil	2 Tbsp. balsamic vinegar
2 garlic cloves, minced	1 (4-oz.) package crumbled feta cheese
1 cup chopped seeded tomato	

1. Prepare green beans according to package directions.

2. Heat oil in a large skillet over medium-high heat. Add garlic; sauté 30 seconds. Add green beans and tomato; cook 1 minute, stirring often, until tomato begins to soften. Add salt, pepper, and vinegar; cook, stirring often, 2 minutes. Remove from heat; sprinkle with cheese.

From My Kitchen
Use ripe in-season tomatoes for best results. During winter months, use a can of drained, diced tomatoes instead.

Herbed Lima Beans

MAKES: 4 SERVINGS   **HANDS-ON TIME:** 5 MIN.
TOTAL TIME: 15 MIN.

1	(16-oz.) package frozen baby lima beans	¼	cup chopped green onions
2	Tbsp. butter	2	tsp. chopped fresh rosemary
¼	cup chopped fresh flat-leaf parsley	½	tsp. table salt
		¼	tsp. freshly ground pepper

1. Prepare lima beans in a saucepan according to package directions. Drain; return to pan. Add butter and remaining ingredients, stirring until butter melts.

Make It A Meal
Serve this simple dish with pork chops and mashed potatoes.

Bacon and Onion Squash Sauté

MAKES: 3 servings   **HANDS-ON TIME:** 18 min.
TOTAL TIME: 18 min.

Serve this quick and easy side dish straight from the skillet.

3	hickory-smoked bacon slices	¼	tsp. table salt
3	cups sliced yellow squash (¾ lb.)	¼	tsp. freshly ground pepper
		¼	cup (1 oz.) freshly shredded Parmesan cheese
¾	cup chopped onion	1	tsp. chopped fresh thyme

1. Cook bacon in a large skillet over medium heat 5 to 7 minutes or until crisp; remove bacon, and drain on paper towels, reserving 1 Tbsp. drippings in skillet. Crumble bacon.

2. Increase heat to medium-high. Sauté squash and onion in hot drippings 6 to 8 minutes or until tender. Remove from heat; sprinkle with salt, pepper, and Parmesan cheese; stir until cheese melts. Sprinkle with bacon and thyme.

Budget Special
Substitute zucchini for the yellow squash, if that's what you have on hand.

Roasted Beets with Goat Cheese

MAKES: 6 servings   **HANDS-ON TIME:** 13 min.
TOTAL TIME: 1 hour, 3 min.

Marcona almonds are a Spanish variety that is usually lightly fried in oil. Find them near the specialty cheeses at your local grocery store.

3	lb. fresh beets (6 medium)	¼	tsp. freshly ground pepper
2	Tbsp. olive oil	2	oz. honey-flavored goat cheese, crumbled
1	tsp. chopped fresh rosemary	¼	cup chopped Marcona almonds*
¼	tsp. table salt		

1. Preheat oven to 450°. Trim beet stems to 1 inch. Gently wash beets; peel and cut into wedges. Place beets in a single layer in a shallow 17- x 12-inch pan or shallow roasting pan. Drizzle beets with olive oil. Sprinkle with rosemary, salt, and pepper, tossing to coat.

2. Bake, uncovered, at 450° for 50 minutes or until beets are tender, turning after 30 minutes.

3. Place beets in a serving bowl; sprinkle with cheese and almonds. Serve immediately.

*Whole blanched almonds may be substituted.

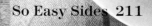

From My Kitchen

Vary flavor by substituting feta cheese or plain goat cheese for the honey-goat cheese.

Smoky Sweet Potato Mash

MAKES: 4 SERVINGS   **HANDS-ON TIME:** 10 MIN.
TOTAL TIME: 23 MIN.

1½ lb. sweet potatoes (3 medium)	½ tsp. smoked paprika
¼ cup butter, melted	¼ tsp. table salt
¼ cup firmly packed light brown sugar	4 cooked and crumbled bacon slices

1. Pierce sweet potatoes several times with a fork; arrange in a circle on paper towels in microwave oven.

2. Microwave at HIGH 8 minutes or until done; let stand 10 to 12 minutes, or until cool to touch.

3. Peel potatoes, and mash with a potato masher until smooth. (Do not use an electric mixer or food processor.) Stir in butter and next 3 ingredients. Sprinkle evenly with crumbled bacon. Serve immediately.

From My Kitchen
Adjust the cooking time as needed for larger or smaller sweet potatoes.

Mediterranean Roasted Potato Salad

MAKES: 6 SERVINGS   **HANDS-ON TIME:** 5 MIN.
TOTAL TIME: 30 MIN.

A great make-ahead side for an outdoor family picnic, this colorful, roasted potato salad inspired by Mediterranean flavors can be served warm or at room temperature.

2	lb. assorted baby potatoes	2	Tbsp. drained capers, coarsely chopped
3	Tbsp. olive oil, divided		
½	tsp. sea salt	8	pitted Spanish olives, sliced
¼	tsp. freshly ground pepper	3	cups loosely packed arugula
I	large lemon		

1. Preheat oven to 450°. Cut smaller potatoes into halves; larger ones into quarters. Place potatoes in a large bowl; drizzle with I Tbsp. olive oil. Sprinkle with salt and pepper, tossing well. Arrange potatoes in a single layer on a jelly-roll pan.

2. Bake at 450° for 25 minutes or until golden brown and tender, stirring halfway through.

3. Meanwhile, grate zest from lemon to equal 1½ tsp. Cut lemon in half; squeeze juice from lemon into a measuring cup to equal 2 Tbsp.

4. Stir together lemon zest, lemon juice, capers, olives, and remaining 2 Tbsp. olive oil in a large bowl. Add potatoes and arugula, tossing to coat. Serve immediately.

Budget Special

Substitute small red potatoes for the more expensive assorted-variety baby potatoes.

Bacon, Tomato, and Blue Cheese Slaw

MAKES: 6 to 8 servings   **HANDS-ON TIME:** 7 min.
TOTAL TIME: 7 min.

Inspired by the classic wedge salad, this slaw combines all our favorite flavors: smoky bacon, sweet tomatoes, and bold blue cheese.

3   Tbsp. white balsamic
    vinegar
2   Tbsp. olive oil
2   tsp. sugar
½   tsp. salt
¼   tsp. freshly ground pepper
1   (16-oz.) package shredded
    coleslaw mix
8   cooked bacon slices,
    crumbled
1   lb. assorted heirloom
    tomatoes, coarsely
    chopped
1   (3-oz.) wedge blue cheese,
    crumbled

From My Kitchen
Purchase a wedge of blue cheese, and crumble it yourself for best flavor; precrumbled blue cheese is not as flavorful.

1. Whisk together first 5 ingredients in a large bowl. Add coleslaw mix and remaining ingredients, tossing to coat. Serve immediately.

Greek Couscous

MAKES: 6 SERVINGS **HANDS-ON TIME: 2 MIN.**
TOTAL TIME: 7 MIN.

Use whole wheat couscous instead of plain to make this a hearty whole grain side dish.

¾ cup uncooked plain couscous

1 cup chopped peeled cucumber

1 cup cherry tomatoes, halved

¼ cup Greek salad dressing

20 pitted kalamata olives

1. Prepare couscous according to package directions. Add cucumber and remaining ingredients, tossing to coat.

• Note: We tested with Ken's Steak House Greek Salad Dressing.

Summer Fresh Ratatouille

MAKES: 6 SERVINGS **HANDS-ON TIME: 20 MIN.**
TOTAL TIME: 20 MIN.

Make It A Meal
Toss this tasty vegetable dish with cooked pasta for an easy meatless main dish.

⅓	cup olive oil
2½	Tbsp. balsamic vinegar
1¼	tsp. garlic salt
½	tsp. freshly ground pepper
4	medium tomatoes (1½ lb.), halved
2	medium zucchini, halved lengthwise
1	medium eggplant, cut into ½-inch-thick slices
1	medium-size red bell pepper, quartered and seeded
⅓	cup chopped fresh basil

1. Preheat grill to 350° to 400° (medium-high heat). Combine first 4 ingredients in a large bowl. Add tomatoes and next 3 ingredients; toss to coat.

2. Remove vegetables from dressing with a slotted spoon, reserving dressing.

3. Grill zucchini, eggplant, and bell pepper, covered with grill lid, 6 minutes on each side or until blistered. Grill tomato halves, covered with grill lid, 2 to 3 minutes on each side or until blistered. Remove vegetables from grill; coarsely chop. Return vegetables to reserved dressing in bowl. Add basil; toss gently. Serve warm.

Rosemary-Garlic White Bean Mash

MAKES: 4 SERVINGS **HANDS-ON TIME:** 11 MIN.
TOTAL TIME: 11 MIN.

1	Tbsp. olive oil
2	garlic cloves, minced
2	(15.8-oz.) cans great Northern beans, drained and rinsed

¼	cup sour cream
1	tsp. chopped fresh rosemary
½	tsp. lemon zest
½	tsp. table salt
¼	tsp. freshly ground pepper

1. Heat oil in a medium nonstick skillet over medium heat. Add garlic; sauté 30 seconds. Add beans; sauté 3 minutes or until thoroughly heated. Remove skillet from heat. Coarsely mash beans with a potato masher or fork. Stir in sour cream, next 4 ingredients, and 2 Tbsp. water.

2. Reduce heat to medium-low; return skillet to heat. Cook, stirring constantly, 2 minutes or until beans are thoroughly heated.

From My Kitchen
Use cannellini beans instead of the great Northern beans, if you'd like.

3-Ingredient Desserts

Whip up a rich
and delicious sweet ending
to your weeknight meal.

Icebox Eclair Pie

MAKES: 12 SERVINGS   **HANDS-ON TIME:** 6 MIN.
TOTAL TIME: 8 HOURS, 6 MIN.

13½ graham cracker sheets
3 (15.5-oz.) packages refriger-
    ated vanilla pudding cups

1 (16-oz.) container ready-
   to-spread rich and creamy
   chocolate frosting

1. Arrange 4½ graham cracker sheets in bottom of an 8-inch square pan. Spread pudding from 5 pudding cups over crackers. Repeat layers once, reserving remaining 2 pudding cups for another use. Layer remaining 4½ graham cracker sheets on top of pudding as above.

2. Place frosting in a microwave-safe bowl. Microwave at HIGH 30 seconds or until pourable, stirring at 15-second intervals. Pour frosting over graham crackers, spreading to edges of pan. Cover and freeze 8 hours. Cut into 12 bars.

• Note: We tested with Betty Crocker Rich and Creamy Chocolate Frosting.

Budget Special

Make your own pudding from a mix rather than using individual pudding cups here, if that's what you have on hand.

Blueberry Yogurt Pops

MAKES: 4 SERVINGS　　**HANDS-ON TIME: 5 MIN.**
TOTAL TIME: 6 HOURS, 5 MIN.

Using whole buttermilk makes a rich and creamy flavor.

¾ cup buttermilk

¼ cup wild blueberry preserves

1 (6-oz.) container wild blueberry Greek yogurt

1. Stir together all ingredients in a 2-cup glass measuring cup. Pour into 4 (3-oz.) popsicle molds. Freeze 6 hours or until firm.

• Note: We tested with Smucker's blueberry preserves and Liberté Wild Blueberry Greek Yogurt.

Lemon Bars

MAKES: 16 SERVINGS   **HANDS-ON TIME:** 8 MIN.
TOTAL TIME: 1 HOUR, 40 MIN.

1   (16.5-ounce) package refrig-   Powdered sugar
     erated sugar cookie dough
1   (10-oz.) jar commercial
     lemon curd

1. Preheat oven to 350°. Crumble two-thirds of cookie dough into an ungreased 9-inch square pan. Press dough together in bottom of pan to form a crust.

2. Bake at 350° for 12 minutes or until light golden brown.

3. Spoon lemon curd evenly over crust. Crumble remaining one-third of cookie dough over lemon curd. Bake at 350° for 20 more minutes or until edges are lightly browned. Cool completely in pan on a wire rack (about 1 hour). Sprinkle with powdered sugar. Cut into 16 bars.

• Note: We tested with Pillsbury Sugar Cookie Dough.

From My Kitchen
Spoon powdered sugar into a fine wire-mesh strainer for even sprinkling over bars.

Raspberry Jammers

MAKES: 1 DOZEN   **HANDS-ON TIME:** 5 MIN.
TOTAL TIME: 20 MIN.

1   (16-oz.) package ready-to-bake sugar cookies

¼   cup raspberry jam

½   cup semisweet chocolate morsels

1. Preheat oven to 350°. Prepare cookies according to package directions. Transfer to a wire rack. Spoon ½ tsp. jam on flat side of each of 12 cookies. Top with remaining cookies, flat side down, gently pressing to spread jam almost to edges.

2. Place chocolate morsels in a small bowl. Microwave at HIGH for 30 seconds to 1 minute or until melted. Place chocolate in a 1-qt. zip-top plastic freezer bag. Snip 1 corner of bag to make a small hole. Gently squeeze bag to drizzle chocolate over tops of cookie sandwiches.

• Note: We tested with Pillsbury Ready To Bake! Sugar Cookies.

From My Kitchen

Use your favorite jam in the centers of these sweet little sandwiches to change the flavor.

Vanilla Wafer Sandwich Bites

MAKES: 2½ DOZEN **HANDS-ON TIME:** 11 MIN.
TOTAL TIME: 1 HOUR, 11 MIN.

⅔ cup creamy peanut butter
60 vanilla wafers

1 (4-oz.) semisweet chocolate
baking bar, chopped

1. Spread about 1 tsp. peanut butter on flat side of each of 30 vanilla wafers. Top with remaining 30 vanilla wafers, flat side down. Place on parchment paper-lined baking sheet. Freeze 30 minutes.

2. Place chocolate in a microwave-safe bowl. Microwave at HIGH 1 minute or until melted, stirring after 30 seconds.

3. Dip half of each cookie sandwich into melted chocolate mixture. Chill 30 minutes or until chocolate is set.

• Note: We tested with Ghirardelli Semi-Sweet Chocolate Baking Bar.

From My Kitchen

Make this simple dessert ahead of time and store in separate bags so you can pull a handful out at a time for a quick snack.

Cinnamon Apple Tarts

MAKES: 1 DOZEN **HANDS-ON TIME:** 10 MIN.
TOTAL TIME: 30 MIN.

Serve with ice cream and caramel topping, if desired.

- 1 (17.3-oz.) package frozen puff pastry sheet, thawed
- 1 (12-oz.) package frozen harvest apples, thawed
- 2 Tbsp. bottled cinnamon sugar

1. Preheat oven to 425°. Cut each puff pastry sheet into 6 rectangles. Spoon 2 Tbsp. apples into center of each rectangle. Pull corners together over apples, pinching edges to seal. Place on a baking sheet lined with parchment paper. Sprinkle each tart with ½ tsp. cinnamon sugar.

2. Bake at 425° for 20 minutes or and until golden brown. Serve immediately.

• Note: We tested with Stouffer's Harvest Apples.

From My Kitchen

Make your own cinnamon sugar: Whisk together 6 Tbsp. sugar and 1½ tsp. ground cinnamon in a small bowl. Store in an airtight container.

Blackberry Bars

MAKES: 2 DOZEN   **HANDS-ON TIME: 11 MIN.**
TOTAL TIME: 2 HOURS, 1 MIN.

2	cups all-purpose flour	2	large eggs
½	cup sugar	1	cup seedless blackberry
¾	cup cold butter, cut up		preserves
¾	cup sugar		
2	(8-oz.) packages cream cheese, softened		

1. Preheat oven to 350°. Combine first 2 ingredients in a large bowl. Cut butter into flour mixture with a pastry blender or fork until crumbly; press in bottom of a lightly greased 13- x 9-inch pan.

2. Bake at 350° for 20 minutes or until golden brown.

3. Meanwhile, place ¾ cup sugar and cream cheese in bowl of a heavy-duty electric stand mixer. Beat at medium speed until fluffy. Add eggs, one at a time, beating just until blended after each addition.

4. Remove pan from oven, and spread preserves evenly over crust. Carefully pour cream cheese mixture over preserves, spreading to edges of pan.

5. Bake at 350° for 30 more minutes or until cheesecake layer is set in center. Cool completely in pan on a wire rack (about 1 hour). Cut into 24 bars.

From My Kitchen
These simple blackberry bars can be made ahead of time and stored in the refrigerator.

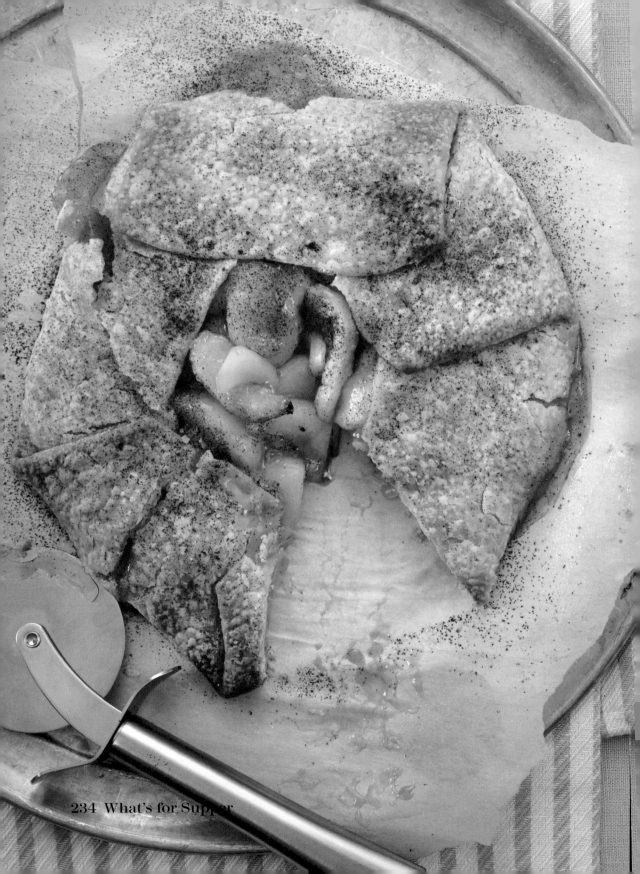

Caramel Apple Gallete

MAKES: 8 SERVINGS **HANDS-ON TIME:** 5 MIN.
TOTAL TIME: 30 MIN.

This could not be easier. Baking on parchment paper makes for easy cleanup.

½ (14.1-oz.) package refriger-   ¼ cup caramel ice cream
   ated piecrusts   topping
1 (21-oz.) can apple pie filling

1. Preheat oven to 425°. Line a large baking sheet with parchment paper. Roll dough into a 13-inch circle on prepared parchment.

2. Place apple filling in center of dough, leaving a 3-inch border. Fold edges of dough toward center, pressing gently to seal (dough will only partially cover apple mixture).

3. Bake at 425° for 25 minutes or until golden brown (filling may leak slightly during cooking).

4. Place caramel topping in a microwave-safe bowl. Microwave at HIGH 20 seconds or until warm. Drizzle galette with caramel topping, and serve warm.

From My Kitchen
Cut with a pizza cutter for easy slicing.

Cream-Filled Pound Cake

MAKES: 4 SERVINGS **HANDS-ON TIME:** 10 MIN.
TOTAL TIME: 10 MIN.

| 4 | Tbsp. pineapple cream cheese, whipped | Sweetened whipped cream |
| 8 | (½-inch-thick) slices pound cake | Fresh strawberries, raspberries and blueberries, mint leaves |

1. Preheat grill to 350° to 400° (medium-high) heat. Spread pineapple cream cheese evenly over 1 side of 4 pound cake slices. Top with remaining 4 pound cake slices.

2. Grill, covered with grill lid, 2 to 3 minutes on each side. Top with whipped cream, berries, and mint leaves. Serve immediately.

From My Kitchen

Choose homemade, frozen, or fresh store-bought cake for this recipe.

S'more Puffs

MAKES: 12 SERVINGS **HANDS-ON TIME:** 5 MIN.
TOTAL TIME: 12 MIN.

12	round buttery crackers	6	large marshmallows,
12	milk chocolate kisses		cut in half

1. Preheat oven to 350°. Place crackers on baking sheet. Top each with 1 milk chocolate kiss and 1 marshmallow half, cut side down.

2. Bake at 350° for 8 minutes or just until marshmallows begin to melt. Cool on a wire rack 5 minutes.

From My Kitchen
"Line the baking sheet with aluminum foil for easy cleanup.

Brownie Buttons

MAKES: 20 SERVINGS **HANDS-ON TIME:** 10 MIN.
TOTAL TIME: 29 MIN.

1 (18.4-oz.) brownie mix
1 bag of assorted miniature
   peanut butter cup candies
   and chocolate-coated
   caramels

1. Preheat oven to 350°. Prepare brownie mix as directed.

2. Spray miniature (1¾") muffin pans with cooking spray, or line pans with paper liners and spray liners with cooking spray. Spoon brownie batter evenly into each cup, filling almost full. Bake at 350° for 19 to 20 minutes. Cool in pans 3 to 4 minutes, and then gently press a miniature candy into each baked brownie until the top of candy is level with top of brownie. Cool 10 minutes in pans. Gently twist each brownie to remove from pan. Cool on a wire rack.

Budget Special
You can also use peanut butter cups or plain caramels, if that's what you have on hand.

Molten Hazelnut Brownies

MAKES: 4 SERVINGS **HANDS-ON TIME: 5 MIN.**
TOTAL TIME: 30 MIN.

| 1 | cup hazelnut spread | 2 | large eggs, beaten |
| ⅔ | cup all-purpose flour | ½ | cup caramel topping |

1. Preheat oven to 350°. Stir together first 3 ingredients in a medium bowl. Divide batter evenly among 4 greased muffin cups. (Muffin cups will be full.)

2. Bake at 350° for 15 minutes or until a wooden pick inserted in center comes out with a few moist crumbs. Cool in pan 10 minutes; carefully remove from muffin cups. Serve warm or cool. Drizzle each brownie with 2 Tbsp. caramel topping just before serving.

• Note: We tested with Nutella hazelnut spread.

From My Kitchen
Serve these quick, gooey-centered brownies with ice cream for a scrumptious treat.

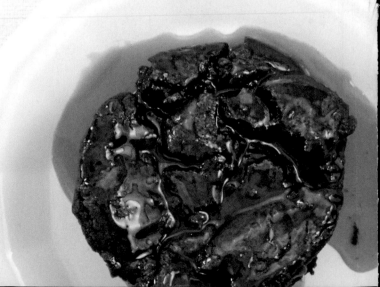

Chocolate-Cherry Crunch

MAKES: 18 SERVINGS **HANDS-ON TIME:** 6 MIN.
TOTAL TIME: 36 MIN.

| 1 | (10-oz.) package bitter-sweet chocolate morsels | ½ | cup chopped dried tart cherries* |
| 3 | cups honey-nut corn flakes cereal, coarsely crushed | | |

1. Place chocolate morsels in a medium microwave-safe bowl. Microwave at HIGH 1 to 1½ minutes or until melted, stirring at 30-second intervals. Stir in cereal and cherries. Using a 1½-inch scoop, drop chocolate mixture in 18 mounds onto a baking sheet lined with parchment paper.

2. Chill 30 minutes or until chocolate is set.

*Sweetened dried cranberries may be substituted.

From My Kitchen

If you don't have a cookie scoop, place 2 Tbsp. mixture in each mound.

Mint Chocolate Truffles

MAKES: 22 TRUFFLES **HANDS-ON TIME:** 13 MIN.
TOTAL TIME: 1 HOUR, 13 MIN.

1 (8-oz.) package cream
   cheese, softened
1 (15.25-oz.) package mint
   cream-filled chocolate
   sandwich cookies, finely
   crushed

2 (4-oz.) bars semisweet
   baking chocolate, chopped

1. Beat cream cheese at low speed with a heavy-duty electric stand mixer fitted with paddle attachment. Stir in crushed cookies. Shape mixture into 1½-inch balls using a small ice-cream scoop; place on a baking sheet lined with parchment paper. Freeze 30 minutes.

2. Place chocolate in a 2-cup glass measuring cup. Microwave at HIGH 1 to 1½ minutes or until melted, stirring at 30-second intervals.

3. Dip balls into chocolate to coat using a fork; tap to remove excess. Return to parchment-lined baking sheet. Chill 30 minutes. Cover and store in refrigerator.

• Note: We tested with Nabisco Oreos Chocolate Cool Mint Creme sandwich cookies.

From My Kitchen
Vary the flavor by using different flavored sandwich cookies.

Chocolate Fondue

**MAKES: 6 to 8 servings   HANDS-ON TIME: 10 min.
TOTAL TIME: 10 min.**

1	cup whipping cream
3	(4-oz.) semisweet choco-late bars, chopped
2	Tbsp. coffee liqueur or other flavored liqueur

1. Microwave whipping cream and chocolate in a microwave-safe glass bowl at HIGH 1½ to 2 minutes, stirring every 30 seconds. Stir in liqueur.

2. Transfer to a fondue pot; keep warm, stirring occasionally. Serve with cookies, pretzels, fruit, and marshmallows.

From My Kitchen
Stir in additional heated whipping cream, 1 tablespoon at a time, if you want a thinner fondue.